When our grandmothers cooked in Provence

The publisher wishes to thank
"Les Olivades", for the cover design,
which is part of the **Bonis** collection.

© ÉDITIONS ÉQUINOXE
Domaine de Fontgisclar, Draille de Magne
13570 Barbentane, France

ISBN 2-84135-123-8

ISSN 1276-4416

When our grandmothers cooked in Provence

Frédérique Féraud-Espérandieu

Illustrations by Cécile Colombo

TRANSLATION BY JULIE ROSSINI

TYPOGRAPHY AND MAKING UP BY YVES PERROUSSEAUX

ÉQUiN●XE

Foreword

*B*orn in Provence, in a wine-growers family, I learnt from my childhood how to know and enjoy the inseparable worlds of wine and gastronomy. Good food, always respected at home, was the preserve of my elders, who helped me discover, very early on, what the charms of Provencal cuisine were. How was I not to share their passion for the art and the pleasures of cooking?

It was by watching them cooking with loving care our traditional family meals that I naturally absorbed, throughout the seasons and the years, the composed and methodical gestures of my mother, grandmothers and aunts.

They confided to me or bequeathed to me a few ancestral secrets, in the yellowed pages of old cooking notebooks, which were intended to highlight the subtle and aromatic tastes of the Provencal products. It seems that the know-how and dexterity are sometimes a matter of magic, but it is nevertheless necessary to know what the principles of the art of cooking are.

Hoping to pass on this modest legacy, I hope that my children, my friends and all lovers of gastronomy will discover in this work a few rules of Provencal cuisine, as well as a number of recipes. Some of them are new, others are traditional, and some have been interpreted with a hint of modernity. This perpetual evolution of cuisine towards new concept of preparation often brightens certain products with a new lightness and fineness of taste.

Let us not forget however, that Provencal cuisine is made of nuances and that it is important not to betray the balance of the rural flavours on the plate. All the recipes that are suggested here are simple and easy to make, but all have a slight touch of elegance and refinement as this is the way that I like to entertain the ones I love.

Menu

EGGS, PASTA & CHEESE

FISH & SEAFOOD

MEATS & POULTRY

SAUCES

DESSERTS PUDDINGS

Soups

Aigo boulido

Preparation time :
10 minutes
Cuisson time : 15 minutes
and 10 minutes for
the infusion

Ingredients for 6 :
1,5 l to 2 l/3 to 4 Pt
of water,
6 cloves of garlic,
2 sage leaves,
1 bay leaf,
1 twig of thyme,
24 slices of toasted baguette,
1 bowl of grated cheese,
Olive oil,
Salt
and freshly ground pepper.

In a saucepan full of boiling water, place the peeled garlic, the thyme, the sage and the bay leaves, with 2 tablespoons of olive oil, some salt and pepper, and cook for 15 minutes.

Remove the saucepan from the heat, cover, leave to infuse for 10 minutes and check the seasoning.

Meanwhile, place the toasted slices of baguette (which you can rub with garlic if you like) in the plates. Pour a dash of olive oil over them, sprinkle a little grated cheese and pour the bouillon on each plate.

This light soup is often served on the day after a holiday because of its digestive virtues. The Provencal name *aigo boulido* means boiled water.

Bouillabaisse

Preparation time : 1 h 30
Cooking time : 30 minutes

Ingredients for 6 :
About 2 1/4 Pt of water
3 kg/6,5 lb of fish for a bouillabaisse (scorpion fish, bass, gur-
nard, monkfish, conger, dory,
rainbow wrasse…, 4 or 5 different species are fine)
2 sliced onions
2 white part of leeks, chopped
3 big tomatoes, ripe
1 stick of green celery
Olive oil
Fennel, parsley, bay leaves,
thyme and saffron
Chilli peppers
The peel of an orange
24 toasted slices of baguette
10 cloves of garlic
1 bowl of aïoli
(about 250 g/1 oz)
1 tea cup of rouille
The aïoli and rouille recipes
are in the *sauces* chapter.

Scale and gut the fish and place them in a dish, separa-
ting the fish with a crumbly flesh, which will constitute
the base for the soup, and the fish with a firmer flesh,
which will be cooked later in the bouillon.

Steam the onions, the leeks, the seeded tomatoes, the
celery, the orange peel and 5 crushed garlic cloves, with
7 or 8 tablespoons of olive oil for about ten minutes. Add
the rockfish, the scorpion fish, and the other fish which
make the "fond" (the base) of the soup.

Add some hot water, one bay leaf, the fennel, some
parsley, two pinches of saffron, and of Cayenne pepper, salt
and pepper. Cook for 8 minutes after it boils.

Remove the fish with a skimmer, use a potato masher
so as to squeeze out all its juices, which you should pour
again in the bouillon. Boil the stock and then add the rest
of the fish. Leave to cook for about ten minutes.

Place all the fish carefully on a dish, and pour the stock
over the toasted slices of bread on each plate. Serve with
the aïoli and the rouille.

This regional dish is always very effective. Be methodical, and it should taste great.

Bourride

**Preparation time :
40 minutes
Cooking time : 30 minutes**

Ingredients for 6 :
2 l of water
2 kg of fish (angler, whiting,
bass, gilt-head, and shellfish if
you like)
1 big onion
The white part of 2 leeks
1 carrot
6 potatoes
The quarter of a fennel
Parsley
A piece of the peel of an
orange (about 5 or 6 cm long)
3 egg yolks
3 dl of dry white wine
Olive oil
1 bowl of aïoli (see the *sauces*
chapter)
1 bouquet garni
Salt
Freshly ground pepper.

Scale, gut and clean the fish, and cut them into sections. In a saucepan, put the onion, the carrot, the chopped leeks, the fennel, the parsley, the bouquet garni, as well as the peel of orange, and place the fish on top. Season with salt and pepper, add the white wine, the hot water and 3 tablespoons of olive oil. Boil, and cook for 15 to 20 minutes.

Remove the fish and the vegetables, and keep them warm. Simmer the stock to reduce it for 10 minutes, and put it through the strainer.

In a bowl, whip 3 egg yolks with a tablespoon of aïoli per guest, and pour it little by little in the stock, stirring constantly with a wooden spoon. Simmer it until it thickens a little and sticks to the spoon. Don't let it boil.

Serve the fish on a dish, pour the soup in the bowls and serve, at the same time, the boiled potatoes and the rest of the aïoli.

This soup is served as a main meal, and should be followed by a light dessert, such as a fruit ice cream, to end the meal.

Consommé de poivrons rouges
Red pepper consommé

Preparation time :
10 minutes
Cooking time : 25 minutes

Ingredients for 6 :
1/2 to 3/4 l/1 Pt to1,5 Pt of water
6 big red peppers
6 tablespoons of olive oil
20 g/1 oz of butter
2 to 3 tablespoons of crème fraîche or double cream
1 teaspoon of sugar
Tabasco
4 pinches of chopped chives
Freshly ground pepper.

Clean the peppers, seed and dice them, and brown them in a saucepan with a little butter and olive oil. Season with salt and pepper, and add the water.

Cook on a brisk heat for 20 to 25 minutes.

Pour this preparation in a food processor with the cream, the teaspoon of sugar and 6 or 7 drops of tabasco. Blend, and check the seasoning.

This soup is really easy to make, and can be served warm or chilled with the sprinkled chives.

Soupe à l'oseille
Sorrel soup

Preparation time :
25 minutes
Cooking time : 35 minutes

Ingredients for 6 :
1.5 to 2 l/3 to 4 Pt of water
500 g/1 lb of fresh sorrel
4 medium-sized potatoes
1 pinch of fresh chervil
1 pinch of ground nutmeg
2 egg yolks
25 g/1 oz of butter
3 tablespoons of crème
fraîche or double cream
Salt
Freshly ground pepper.

Clean the sorrel, remove the ribs, wash thoroughly, and strain well. Brown it in a saucepan with 2 tablespoons of butter, some salt and pepper and a pinch of ground nutmeg, for 4 or 5 minutes. Put to one side.

Boil the water with some salt and pepper, add the potatoes, cut into pieces and, 25 minutes later, add the sorrel and leave to cook for 10 minutes.

Remove the soup from the heat, mix it with the egg yolks and the cream, and put it through the food processor. Check the seasoning.

This soup is served warm, with a pinch of chopped chervil on top.

Fresh sorrel is not always easily found on the market place. You can buy a large quantity during the right season and sweat it in a saucepan with a little water for 3 or 4 minutes. Strain it and freeze it.

Courge

Soupe au pistou
Pesto soup

Preparation time : 45 mn
Cooking time : 1 h 15 mn

Ingredients for 6 :
2,5 l/5 pt of water
100 to 150 g/3,5 to 5 oz
of salted pork or fresh belly
of pork
1 big onion
4 big ripe tomatoes
4 small courgettes/zucchinis
2 leeks
1 stick of celery
2 handfuls of green beans
3 potatoes
100 to 150 g/3,5 to 5 oz
of fresh white beans
Grated cheese
Olive oil
Salt
Freshly ground pepper

For the pesto :
60 to 70 g/2 to 2,5 oz of basil
leaves
3 cloves of garlic
Olive oil
Salt
Freshly ground pepper.

Dice all the vegetables (about 1 square cm), or cut them into small sticks (about 2 cm long), according to their form.

Slice the onion and brown it in a large saucepan with the salted pork and 2 to 3 tablespoons of olive oil. Add the seeded tomatoes, some salt and pepper, and cook for a few minutes. Add about 2 l of cold water and the white beans. Boil for another 15 minutes, and add the green beans, the potatoes, the leeks, the stick of celery and finally the courgettes. Season, and leave to cook slowly for one hour.

Meanwhile, blend the three garlic cloves with the basil leaves, a pinch of cooking salt, a pinch of pepper, 6 tablespoons of olive oil, and three of bouillon. This thin pommade constitutes the pesto.

Blend the soup and the pesto in the tureen, and check the seasoning. You might serve it accompanied with a separate bowl of grated cheese.

This soup is essentially served in the South of France, but it deserves to be known. It will be especially delicious in Spring, when vegetables are very tender.

Soupe de courges
Marrow/squash soup

Preparation time :
20 minutes
Cooking time : 30 minutes

Ingredients for 6 :
3/4 l/1,5 Pt of water
3/4 l/1,5 Pt of chicken stock
1,5 kg/3,5 lb
of marrow/squash
1 pinch of sugar
1 bay leaf
4 to 5 tablespoons of crème
fraîche or double cream
80 g/3 oz of butter
Salt
Freshly ground pepper.

Peel and roughly dice the marrow. Drop the marrow in the water and the stock. Season with the salt and pepper, the bay leaf and the whole peeled garlic cloves, and leave to cook for 30 minutes after it comes to the boil.

Put the soup through the food processor with the sugar, the butter and the cream. Check the seasoning, and, if the soup is too thick, you might want to add a little milk.

This soup is served hot, sprinkled with a little grated cheese if you like.

It is sometimes served in a scooped out marrow. In this case, cut a lid in the marrow, hollow out the flesh, and use it for the soup.

Soupe de moules
Mussel soup

Preparation time :
30 minutes
Cooking time : 35 minutes

Ingredients for 6 :
1,5 l to 2 1/3 to 4 Pt of water
3 1/6 Pt of mussels
1 bouquet garni
2 cloves of garlic
1 leek
1 big onion
1 stick of green celery
3 tomatoes
4 or 5 pinches of saffron
Olive oil
2 dl/0,5 Pt of dry white wine
Salt
Freshly ground pepper.

Clean the mussels and open them, for 8 minutes on a brisk heat, with the white wine and the bouquet garni. Cover the saucepan and stir from time to time.

Remove the mussels with a skimmer, and remove their shells after they have cooled down. Sieve the cooking liquid through a square of muslin, so as to filter any sand which might have stayed in the shells.

Meanwhile, warm 3 or 4 tablespoons of olive oil in a stew pot, add the minced vegetables, the crushed garlic, and brown them on a slow heat. Add 1,5 l of hot water, cook for 15 minutes and put the soup through the food processor.

Pour the stock in a saucepan and add the mussels and their cooking liquid. Add very little salt, as the liquid is already salted, and some pepper, add a pinch of saffron, and cook for 8 to 10 minutes.

Check the seasoning and serve this soup hot or chilled according to the season.

This soup is really tasty. Be very careful when sieving the cooking liquid, so as not to leave any sand. It would be very disagreeable to come across it when savouring the soup.

Soupe de poissons
Fish soup

Preparation time :
25 minutes
Cooking time : 30 minutes

Ingredients for 6 :
2 1/4 Pt of water
2.5 to 3 kg/6 to 6,5 lb of fish
(scorpion fish, weever, gur-
nard, shellfish)
1 leek
1 carrot
1 stick of green celery
2 middle-sized onions
2 tomatoes
5 cloves of garlic
1 twig of fennel
1 pinch of thyme flowers
A small piece of the peel of an
orange (5 or 6 cm long)
4 or 5 pinches of saffron
Olive oil
2 handfuls of large vermicelli,
if you like them
Salt
Freshly ground pepper.

Mince the vegetables, brown them in a stew pot with 6 or 7 tablespoons of olive oil, and add the crushed garlic cloves, the fennel, the bay leaf and the orange-peel. When the vegetables have browned a little, pour in about 2 l of water, and season with salt and pepper.

Leave to cook for 3 or 4 minutes.

Throw the gutted and cleaned fish in the sauce-pan, and leave them to cook for ten minutes after it comes to boil.

Remove them with a skimmer, and use a potato masher so as to squeeze all the juices, which you should pour again in the stock. Add the saffron, leave to simmer for ten more minutes and, if you like, throw in the vermicelli, which you should in this case cook for 8 minutes.

Check the seasoning.

This soup is served hot. You can present it accompanied with aïoli, rouille, and croûtons rubbed with garlic, as for the bouillabaisse.

Vegetables

Artichauts à la barigoule
Artichokes à la barigoule

**Preparation time :
20 minutes
Cooking time : 60 minutes**

Ingredients for 6 :
18 small and fresh artichokes
150 g / 5 oz of salted pork, cut
into strips
2 carrots
2 onions
2 lettuce hearts
1 handful of sorrel
2 handfuls of spinach
3 crushed cloves of garlic
1,5 dl / 1/4 Pt of dry white
wine
1/4 l / 1/2 Pt of stock
Olive oil
Salt
Freshly ground pepper.

Wash the artichokes and remove a few external leaves. In a large saucepan, brown the salted pork, the onions, the salad, the sorrel, the spinach and the carrots, all chopped, for 3 or 4 minutes, with 6 tablespoons of olive oil, on a slow heat.

Add the artichokes, a dash of olive oil, the garlic, the salt and the pepper, and leave to cook for 10 minutes, stirring from time to time.

Pour in the white wine and the stock and let it simmer so that it reduces by half on a brisk heat, and then leave to cook for 45 minutes.

Check the seasoning and serve hot.

Aubergines rôties
Roasted aubergines / eggplants

Preparation time :
25 minutes
Cooking time : 20 minutes

Ingredients for 6 :
1 kg/2 lb of aubergines/egg-plants
1 bowl of coulis de tomates (see in the "sauces" chapter)
5 or 6 pinches of chopped parsley
Some cooking salt
Olive oil
Salt
Freshly ground pepper.

Peel the aubergines and cut them into two length-wise. With the point of a knife, draw a few crosses on their flesh, so that they cook better, sprinkle a little cooking salt over them, and leave them to sweat for 15 minutes in a sieve (it will remove their potential bitterness, and they will also absorb less oil when cooked).

Meanwhile, heat up 1/5 l of oil in a frying pan and fry the aubergines on both sides until they are crisp and brown. Remove them from the frying pan, and drain them in a sieve and with kitchen paper so as to absorb the excess oil.

Lay them on a dish, and pour a layer of coulis over each aubergine and sprinkle with fresh parsley.

This dish can be served cold or warm, according to the season, as a starter, or as an accompaniment of a leg of lamb or a beef rib.

Aubergines à la bohémienne

Aubergines/eggplants à la bohémienne

Preparation time :
30 minutes
Cooking time : 35 minutes

Ingredients for 6 :
6 aubergines/eggplants
6 ripe, peeled and seeded tomatoes
1 crushed clove of garlic
1 onion
Thyme
1 bay leaf
4 twigs of parsley
Olive oil
Grated cheese
Salt
Freshly ground pepper.

Peel the aubergines, and cut them into slices 1,5 cm wide. Heat up half a litre of olive oil in a frying pan and dip the aubergines in the oil as soon as it is hot. When they are brown, drain them, season with salt and pepper and leave to one side.

Meanwhile, brown the minced onion in 3 tablespoons of olive oil for 3 minutes, then add the tomatoes, the garlic, the parsley, a pinch of thyme, some salt and pepper.

Leave this coulis to reduce for about 10 minutes on a brisk heat, and blend the aubergines and the tomatoes together.

Leave to cook once again for 10 minutes, and check the seasoning.

Butter an oven dish, lay down the aubergines and add the grated cheese. Add a few knobs of butter on top and cook it au gratin for 10 to 15 minutes.

Aubergines farcies
Stuffed aubergines / eggplants

Preparation time :
45 minutes
Cooking time : 25 minutes

Ingredients for 6 :
250 g/8 oz of minced meat
(heel of ham, boiled beef or
veal, or roast meat)
1 big onion
2 peeled and seeded tomatoes
1 crushed clove of garlic
1 loaf of sandwich bread or 2
slices of melba toast
5 twigs of parsley
1 pinch of herbes de Provence
2 egg yolks
Olive oil
Salt
Freshly ground pepper.

Cut the unpeeled aubergines into two, lengthwise. With a spoon, hollow out their flesh, trying to leave the skin intact, and leave to one side. Cook the skins for 8 minutes in a microwave, or for 20 minutes in a traditional oven. Lay them in an oven dish and prepare the stuffing.

Brown the minced onion, the raw flesh of the aubergines and the chopped tomatoes with 3 or 4 tablespoons of olive oil in a frying pan for 5 minutes. Add the meat, the garlic, the parsley, the bread or the toast soaked in milk, the salt, the pepper and the aromatic herbs. Stir well, and leave to cook for about 10 minutes. Add the 2 egg yolks, taking care to blend them well with all the other ingredients, and check the seasoning.

Fill in the aubergine skins with this stuffing, add a dash of olive oil and brown in the oven on a medium heat for 25 minutes. This dish can be served either warm or cold, according to the season.

In the *Vegetables* chapter, you will find five different recipes for vegetables cooked in the same way. You can prepare several kinds of these and serve them with rice. It is colourful and very popular.

Beignets de fleurs de courgettes
Courgettes / zucchinis flowers fritters

Preparation time :
15 minutes
Cooking time : 6 minutes
for each fritter

Ingredients for 6 :
18 flowers
of courgettes/zucchinis
1 tablespoon of minced parsley
1 tablespoon of minced chives
Salt
Freshly ground pepper
Frying oil

For the batter :
250 g/8 oz of flour
2 eggs
2 teaspoons of olive oil
2 to 2,5 dl/ 0,5 Pt of water
1 pinch of salt.

Wash the flowers, drain them, and dry them well with kitchen paper. Meanwhile, prepare the batter : in a mixing bowl, pour 250 g of flour, add a pinch of salt, 2 egg yolks, and 2 teaspoons of olive oil.

Mix well, and progressively pour the water, so as to obtain a smooth batter. Add 2 whipped egg whites, just before cooking the fritters.

Dip each flower in the batter and fry it in the hot oil for 4 to 5 minutes, until the fritters are brown.

Lay them on a dish and sprinkle them with minced herbs.

Serve warm. This speciality is from Nice, and it constitutes a starter with a subtle taste.

Take care to order the flowers in the Spring from your greengrocer, as they might prove difficult to find otherwise.

Cardons de Noël
Christmas cardoons

Preparation time :
20 minutes
Cooking time :
about 60 minutes

Ingredients for 6 :
1 kg/2 lb of cardoons, white and tender
3 garlic cloves
3 or 4 pinches
of minced parsley
1 lemon
Butter
Salt
Freshly ground pepper.

Carefully clean the cardoons, taking care to remove the strings, and cut them into pieces of about 4 cm. Heat up 2 l of salted water, throw the cardoons in the boiling water and lemon juice. Leave them to cook for 3/4 of an hour, then strain them.

Melt 2 tablespoons of butter and olive oil in a saucepan to brown the cardoons in for 10 minutes.

Season with salt and pepper, and add the garlic and the parsley as well as half the lemon juice. Serve hot.

This vegetable is especially served in Provence during the Christmas festivities. It is traditionally served with meats, poultry and fish.

Croquettes de pommes de terre à l'ail

Potatoes and garlic croquettes

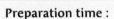

Preparation time :
30 minutes
Cooking time : 35 minutes

Ingredients for 6 :
1 kg/2 lb of potatoes with
floury flesh
8 tablespoons of flour
4 eggs
3 egg yolks
3 crushed garlic cloves
3 or 4 pinches
of minced parsley
1 pinch of ground nutmeg
Sunflower or peanut oil
Bread crumbs
Salt
Freshly ground pepper.

Peel the potatoes, throw them in a saucepan filled with salted and cold water and cook them for 20 minutes after the first boil.

Drain them and use a potato masher so as to make a purée, and dry this purée in a saucepan on a slow heat, season with salt and pepper, and add the nutmeg, the garlic and the minced parsley. Remove from the heat, then add 3 egg yolks, and 2 whole eggs. Stir well, and leave to cool down for a few minutes.

Spread a few tablespoons of flour on a board, and make croquettes in the shape of fingers.

Dip the croquettes in the beaten eggs, and, after rolling them in the bread crumbs, fry them in the hot but not boiling oil until they brown.

Drain them on kitchen paper and serve warm. They make a nice accompaniment for roasted meats and poultry.

Soupe de courges
Marrow/squash soup

Preparation time :
30 minutes
Cooking time : 30 minutes

Ingredients for 6 :
1,5 kg/3 lb of ripe tomatoes
6 eggs
120 g/4 oz of crème fraîche or
double cream
120 g/4 oz grated cheese
30 g/1 oz of soft butter
Salt
Freshly ground pepper.

Peel and seed the tomatoes, and chop them roughly. Sweat them for 15 minutes in a sieve by sprinkling them with a little cooking salt. Put them to one side.

Beat up the eggs with the cream, the softened butter, and the grated cheese, and then add the well drained tomatoes. Delicately blend with a whisk and season strongly with salt and pepper.

Butter 6 individual ramekins, and pour the flan in them. Cook in a bain marie in a hot oven for about 30 minutes.

You should serve the flans warm, and can top them with one or two tablespoons of cold "sauce aux tomates crues", which you can find in the *sauces* chapter.

Flan d'épinards
Spinach flan

Preparation : 10 minutes
Cooking time : 30 minutes

Ingredients for 6 :
300 g/10 oz of spinach,
cooked,
and drained
150 g/5 oz of crème fraîche or
double cream
5 eggs
About 30 g/1 oz of grated
cheese
1 pinch of ground nutmeg
Salt
Freshly ground pepper.

In a mixing bowl, blend the cooked spinach with the beaten eggs, the crème fraîche, the grated cheese, the nutmeg and the salt and pepper.

Pour the preparation in a tin and cook it for about 30 minutes in a hot oven (gas mark 7 or 8). You can check whether it is cooked or not by dipping the point of a knife in the cake; it should come out clean if the flan is cooked. Turn it out, and then slice it.

This spinach flan can be served warm, as a starter, topped with a coulis de tomates or a cream of red peppers (see these recipes in the *sauces* chapter), or cold with mayonnaise.

It can also be presented as an accompaniment for a meat or a grilled fish.

Gâteau de courgettes
Courgette/zucchini cake

Preparation time :
30 minutes
Cooking time : 30 minutes

Ingredients for 6 :
1 kg/2 lb of courgettes/zucchinis
6 peeled and seeded tomatoes
2 middle-sized onions
1 crushed garlic clove
4 eggs
80 g/2,5 oz of grated cheese
3 tablespoons of crème fraîche or double cream
1 pinch of basil
1 pinch of tarragon
1 pinch of mint
1 pinch of oregano
1 teaspoon of sugar
Olive oil
Butter
Salt
Ground pepper.

Peel the courgettes and dice them. Brown them with a minced onion in 3 tablespoons of olive oil and one of butter, some salt and pepper for about 20 minutes on a brisk heat. Stir regularly and add 0,5 l of water if necessary. Reduce the heat at the end of the cooking time, and leave to evaporate the water. Drain the courgettes in a sieve for 10 to 15 minutes, then put to one side.

Whisk the eggs and the grated cheese in a bowl with the salt, the pepper and the cream. Mix in the courgettes.

Butter a tin, pour the preparation in and cook it in the oven for about 30 minutes. At the end of the cooking time, dip the point of a knife in the gâteau, and it should come out clean if it is well cooked.

While the gâteau cooks, sweat in a frying pan an onion with 2 tablespoons of olive oil, add the garlic, the aromatic herbs, the sugar and the salt and pepper. Leave the coulis to reduce for about 10 minutes and put it through the food processor, and put it to one side.

This gâteau of courgettes is served cold, sliced and topped with coulis de tomates. It constitutes a very popular starter. It can also be served without the coulis, as an accompaniment for a roasted meat.

34

TABLE DE NUI

6, courgette

une courgette

Gâteau d'asperges
Asparagus cake

Preparation time :
15 minutes
Cooking time : 1 h 05 mn

Ingredients for 6 :
600 g/1,3 lb of fresh white
asparagus, or, failing that, 350
to 400 g/10 to 15 oz of tinned
asparagus, drained
6 eggs
200 to 250 ml/0,5 Pt of
crème fraîche or double
cream
About 80 g of grated cheese
Salt
Freshly ground pepper.

Peel the asparagus with a potato peeler, and cook them in 1,5 l of salted boiling water for 30 minutes. Drain and put to one side.

Put the asparagus through the food processor with 3 whole eggs, 3 egg yolks, the cream, the grated cheese, the salt and the pepper until it forms a smooth purée.

Butter 6 individual ramekins, and pour the liquid preparation in. Cook the "gâteaux" in a bain marie (place the ramekins on an oven dish, in which you should pour 1/2 l of water, so that the bottoms of the ramekins soak in water) for 35 minutes in a hot oven. To check whether it is cooked or not, dip in the point of a knife, and it is cooked if the knife comes out cleanly.

Leave the ramekins to cool down, then turn them out with the help of a knife and lay the cakes in the plates. Serve warm.

This asparagus gâteau is served as an accompaniment for white or roasted meats. It may also be served as a starter, topped with coulis de tomates, or with « crème de poivrons rouges. » (You can find these recipes in the *sauces* and *vegetables* chapters).

Gratin d'aubergines
Aubergines / eggplants au gratin

Preparation time :
45 minutes
Cooking time : 15 minutes

Ingredients for 6 :
1 kg/2 lb of aubergines/egg-plants
50 g/1,5 oz of butter
4 tablespoons of flour
1/2 l/1 Pt of milk
About 100 g/3,5 oz of grated cheese
Peanut oil
1 pinch of ground nutmeg
Cooking salt
Salt
Freshly ground pepper.

Peel the aubergines and cut them into two, lengthwise. With the point of a knife, draw a few crosses on their flesh, so that they cook better, sprinkle a little cooking salt over them and leave them to sweat for 15 minutes in a sieve (it will remove any potential bitterness).

Heat up the oil in a deep fryer and fry the aubergines on both sides until they brown. Remove them, drain them in a sieve and absorb the excess fat with kitchen paper. Put to one side.

Melt the butter in a saucepan, add the flour, and mix the two ingredients well : there should be no lumps. Pour the milk in little by little and stir, until the sauce thickens a little. Season with salt and pepper and a pinch of ground nutmeg. This constitutes a "sauce béchamel".

Butter an oven dish, lay down the aubergines, and pour the sauce on top. Sprinkle with grated cheese and cook au gratin in a hot oven for about 15 minutes.

This gratin is a perfect accompaniment for a roasted meat.

Gratin de courgettes
Courgettes/zucchinis au gratin

Preparation time :
25 minutes
Cooking time : 45 minutes

Ingredients for 6 :
1,2 kg/2,5 lb of
courgettes/zucchinis
40 g/1,5 oz of butter
4 tablespoons of butter
1/2 l of milk
About 100 g of grated cheese
Olive oil
Ground nutmeg
Salt
Freshly ground pepper.

Peel the courgettes, cut them in 1,5 cm wide slices and brown them in a frying pan with 5 or 6 tablespoons of olive oil until they are brown (about 25 minutes). Season with salt and pepper and drain them in a sieve to remove the excess oil. Put to one side.

Melt the butter in a saucepan, add the flour, and mix the two ingredients well : there should be no lumps. Pour the milk in little by little and stir, until the sauce thickens a little. Season with salt and pepper and a pinch of ground nutmeg. This constitutes a *sauce béchamel.*

Butter an oven dish lay down the courgettes, and pour the sauce on top.

Sprinkle with grated cheese and cook au gratin in a hot oven for about 10 to 15 minutes.

This gratin is served hot with roasted lamb, a fillet roast or a braised fish.

Gratin d'épinards
à l'ail et au persil
Spinach au gratin, with garlic and parsley

Preparation time :
40 minutes
Cooking time : 10 minutes

Ingredients for 6 :
1,5 kg/3,5 lb of fresh spinach
4 crushed garlic cloves
5 pinches of chopped parsley
3 tablespoons of flour
Butter
1/2 l/1 Pt of milk
Nutmeg
Olive oil
Salt
Ground pepper.

Wash the spinach, throw it in salted boiling water and cook for 15 minutes. Drain and squeeze it so as to extract all their water, and chop roughly.

Brown the spinach for 10 minutes in 2 tablespoons of olive oil and 2 of butter and add the garlic, the parsley, the pepper and a pinch of ground nutmeg. Check the seasoning.

Meanwhile, melt 50 g of butter in a saucepan, add the flour and mix the 2 ingredients well : there should be no lumps. Pour the milk little by little until the sauce thickens. Season with salt and pepper and blend the spinach and the béchamel sauce.

Butter an oven dish, pour in the preparation and sprinkle with grated cheese, and brown for 10 minutes in a hot oven.

Mousse d'aubergines
Aubergines / eggplants mousse

Preparation : 15 minutes
Cooking time : 25 minutes

Ingredients for 6 :
1 kg/2 lb of aubergines/egg-plants
2 garlic cloves
1/2 lemon
5 minced mint leaves
10 chopped twigs of chives
2 chopped twigs of dill
Olive oil
Salt
Freshly ground pepper.

Peel the aubergines, dice them and brown them in a saucepan with a little olive oil for about 25 minutes. Season with salt and pepper, stir well and drain in a sieve.

Put the aubergines through the blender with 2 tablespoons of lemon juice, the garlic and the herbs, until you obtain a mousse, and check the seasoning.

This dish can be served warm or chilled, as a snack or an accompaniment for fish or meat.

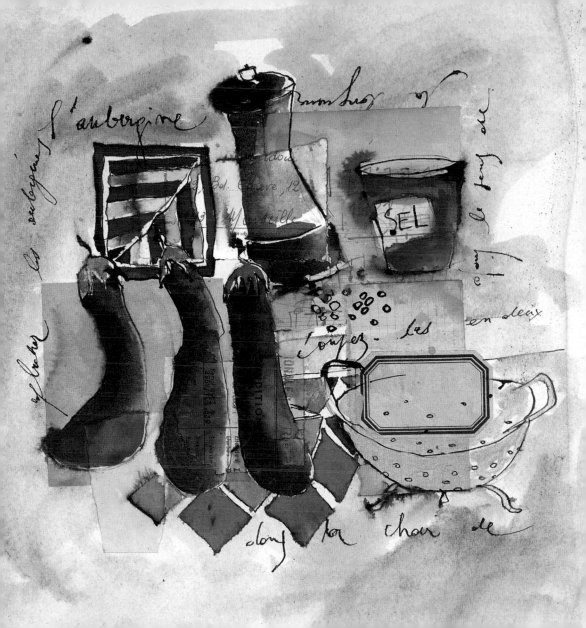

Oignons farcis
Stuffed onions

Preparation time :
35 minutes
Cooking time : 25 minutes

Ingredients for 6 :
8 big white onions
250 g/10 oz of minced meat
(heel of ham, boiled beef or
veal or any roasted meat)
2 peeled and seeded tomatoes
1 crushed clove of garlic
1 slice of sandwich bread or
2 slices of melba toast
1 dl of warm milk
5 twigs of parsley
1 pinch of thyme
1 pinch of chopped basil
leaves
2 egg yolks
Olive oil
Salt
Freshly ground pepper.

Peel the onions, hollow the tender inner flesh out with a spoon and put it away it in a bowl. Blanch the onion «shells» for 5 to 6 minutes in boiling water, or cook them for 8 minutes in the microwave. Lay them in an oven dish and prepare the stuffing as follows.

Brown the onion flesh with the chopped tomatoes in a frying pan with 3 or 4 tablespoons of oil, for 5 minutes, then add the meat, the garlic, the parsley, the bread or the toast soaked in the milk, the salt, the pepper and the aromatic herbs. Stir well and cook for about 10 minutes. Finally, add 2 egg yolks, taking care to blend them well with the other ingredients, and check the seasoning.

Fill the onions with this stuffing, sprinkle with a dash of olive oil and brown them in a hot oven for 25 minutes. You might serve this dish warm or cold.

In the *Vegetables* chapter, you will find five different recipes for vegetables cooked in the same way. You can prepare several kinds of these and serve them with rice. It is colourful and very popular.

Oignons glacés
Glazed onions

Preparation time :
15 minutes
Cooking time : 20 minutes

Ingredients for 6 :
6 onions
1/4 l/1/2 Pt of water
or vegetable stock
1 pinch of sugar
Butter
Salt
Freshly ground pepper.

Peel the onions and slice them finely. Brown the onions in 3 or 4 tablespoons of butter, on a slow heat, in a frying pan, for about 7 or 8 minutes, until they slightly change colour. Add the stock so that the onions are slightly immersed in it.

Cover the frying pan and leave to simmer for about 20 minutes. At the end of the cooking time, add a pinch of sugar. The onions are usually cooked when the stock's consistency is a little syrupy.

The *onions glacés* are served either warm or cold. You can serve them with a pie, a roasted piece of meat, a braised fish or a tureen.

Pan bagnat

**Preparation time :
10 minutes**

Ingredients per person :
2 slices of farmhouse bread
3 fillets of anchovies
4 or 5 slices of onion
1/2 a hard boiled egg, sliced
4 slices of tomato
4 stoned black olives
1/2 garlic clove
A few leaves of fresh basil
A few leaves of fresh mint
Olive oil
Salt
Freshly ground pepper.

Rub the inside of the slices of bread with garlic, pour a dash of olive oil over the inferior slice, and lay down the slices of tomato, the onion, the egg, the anchovies and the olives, as well as the aromatic herbs, and some salt and pepper.

Pour another dash of olive oil, and cover with the second slice of bread so as to finish the sandwich.

Pan bagnat is served chilled. It is an excellent sandwich to take away for a picnic. In this case, don't forget the paper napkins, which might prove very useful.

44

Poivrons confits à l'huile d'olive
Soft peppers in olive oil

Preparation time :
15 minutes
Cooking time : 40 minutes

Ingredients for 6 :
6 peppers (red if possible)
3 garlic cloves
Olive oil
Salt
Freshly ground pepper.

Wash the peppers, remove the stalk and the seeds, and cut them into two, lengthwise. Grill the peppers on an oiled baking tray for about 40 minutes. Peel the peppers and cut them into strips.

Lay them in a hollow recipient with the crushed garlic, the salt and the pepper, and cover them completely with olive oil, so as to let them soak.

This preparation has to be made several hours beforehand, as it is served cool. It can be presented with an omelette, fried eggs or cold meats or with an aperitif.

I would advise you, if you have enough time, to make a good quantity, as they can be preserved for a few days in the fridge.

Poivrons farcis
Stuffed peppers

**Preparation time :
35 minutes
Cooking time : 25 minutes**

Ingredients for 6 :
6 middle-sized peppers, either green or red
250 g/10 oz of minced meat (heel of ham, boiled beef or veal, or any roasted meat)
2 peeled and seeded tomatoes
1 big onion
1 slice of sandwich bread or 2 slices of melba toast
1 dl of warm milk
1 garlic clove
4 twigs of parsley
1 pinch of herbes de Provence
2 egg yolks
Olive oil
Salt
Freshly ground pepper.

Wash the peppers, and remove their tops, and the seeds. Blanch them in 2 l of salted and boiling water for 8 to 10 minutes or cook them for 8 minutes in the microwave. Lay them in a buttered oven dish, ready to be stuffed, and prepare the stuffing as follows.

Brown the minced onion and the chopped tomatoes in a frying pan with 2 tablespoons of olive oil for 3 to 4 minutes, and add the meat, the garlic, the parsley, the sandwich bread soaked in the milk, the salt, the pepper and the herbes de Provence.

Stir well and leave to cook for about 10 minutes. Finally add the 2 egg yolks, and blend them with the other ingredients well. Check the seasoning.

Fill the peppers with this stuffing, sprinkle with a dash of vinegar and brown for 25 minutes in a medium oven. This dish can be served hot or chilled according to the season.

In the *Vegetables* chapter, you will find five different recipes for vegetables cooked in the same way. You can prepare several kinds of these and serve them with rice. It is colourful and very appreciated.

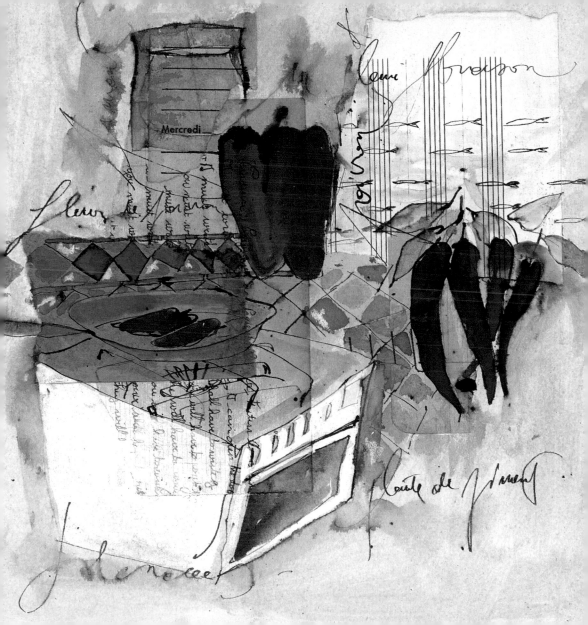

Purée de petits pois frais
Fresh garden peas purée

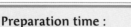

Preparation time :
5 minutes
Cooking time : 20 minutes

Ingredients for 6 :
700 to 800 g/1,5 lb of shelled
high quality garden peas, or,
failing that, high quality frozen peas
1 small onion
120 to 150 g/4 to 5 oz
of crème fraîche
or double cream
150 ml/1/4 Pt of milk
Salt
Freshly ground pepper.

Throw the peas and the onion in a large saucepan filled with salted boiling water and leave them to cook for 20 minutes past the boil when they are fresh, or 15 minutes when frozen.

Drain the peas and the onion, and put them through the food processor with the cream and the pepper, so as to obtain a smooth purée. If the consistency of the purée is too thick, add a glass of milk. Check the seasoning.

This *purée de petits pois* is fine and tasty. It is better served with steamed or roasted fish, poultry and white meats.

Serve hot.

Ratatouille

Preparation time :
30 minutes
Cooking time : 1 hour

Ingredients for 6 :
4 aubergines/eggplants
4 courgettes/zucchinis
4 green peppers
1 kg of ripe tomatoes
2 big onions
3 crushed garlic cloves
1 bay leaf
3 or 4 pinches of minced parsley
1 pinch of ground thyme
A few chopped basil leaves
2 twigs of tarragon
Olive oil
1 handful of stoned green olives («picholine» if you can find them).

Wash the vegetables. Peel and seed the tomatoes, and cut them into 4. Peel the aubergines, as well as the courgettes, and dice them. Seed the peppers, cut them into strips, and slice the onions. Put to one side.

Heat up 6 or 7 tablespoons of olive oil in a frying pan and brown the courgettes on a brisk heat, until they achieve a golden colour. Season with salt and pepper, remove from the heat, and drain.

In the same frying pan, brown the aubergines in the same way, until they are brown too, season, remove from the heat, and drain. Do the same with the peppers.

Finally, sweat the onions in a sauce pan with 3 tablespoons of olive oil, add the tomatoes, the garlic, the thyme, the basil, the bay leaf and the tarragon. Cook uncovered and leave this "coulis" to reduce. Gather all the vegetables in a large saucepan, add the olives, stir well and leave to cook on a very slow heat for about 15 minutes. Check the seasoning, pour the *ratatouille* in a dish and sprinkle with fresh parsley.

This dish can be served warm or chilled, according to the season.

Salade de crudités à l'anchoïade

Crudités salad with anchoïade dressing

Preparation time :
30 minutes

Ingredients for 6 :
1 stick of green celery
1/2 branch of white card
2 hearts of cauliflower
2 carrots
2 spring artichokes
2 tomatoes
1 head of chicory
1/2 pepper
1 head of curly endive
A few heads of young and
fresh spinach
1 bunch of spring onions
1.5 to 2 dl of anchoïade (see
the recipe in the *sauces*
chapter).

Wash the vegetables, peel and clean them, slice them, or cut them into strips or sticks according to their form.

Lay all the raw vegetables in a large salad bowl and sprinkle with the «anchoïade» sauce, also called "pébrade" in the South of France, so as to leave the vegetables well impregnated with it. Stir well, and serve chilled.

You might serve it as a main meal, if you present it with hard-boiled eggs and a few boiled potatoes which harmonize well with *anchoïade*.

Salade de courgettes grillées
Grilled courgettes/zucchinis salad

Preparation time :
15 minutes
Cooking time : 45 minutes

Ingredients for 6 :
1,5 kg/3,5 lb of
courgettes/zucchinis
3 garlic cloves
4 pinches of minced parsley
Olive oil
Salt
Freshly ground pepper.

Peel the courgettes and cut them into slices 1,5 cm wide. Lay them on a baking tray, season with salt and pepper and sprinkle with olive oil. Cook them in a hot oven for 45 minutes, taking care to move them around regularly, so as to leave them brown all over.

Remove from the oven and drain them in a sieve.

Lay them in a hollow dish and sprinkle with 3 to 4 tablespoons of fresh olive oil, blended with the crushed garlic and the parsley. Check the seasoning then place in the fridge.

This salad is served chilled with a roasted piece of meat or as a fresh starter in the summer season. You can also prepare it with other vegetables such as peppers, or aubergines.

Tomates à la provençale

Preparation time :
15 minutes
Cooking time : 40 minutes

Ingredients for 6 :
12 ripe tomatoes
4 garlic cloves
1 bunch of parsley
3 to 4 pinches of thyme
1 tablespoon of sugar
Olive oil
Freshly ground pepper.

Wash the tomatoes, divide them into two width-ways, and seed them. Crush the garlic with a garlic press and mince the parsley.

Butter a baking tray and lay the tomatoes side by side.

Sprinkle with a dash of olive oil, the parsley, the thyme and the sugar, and season with salt and pepper.

Add a dash of olive oil and cook the tomatoes for about 40 minutes in a hot oven until they are brown.

You can serve the *tomates à la provençale* either hot or cold, and you may accompany them with rice.

tomates

Tomates en salade
Tomato salad

Preparation time :
15 minutes

Ingredients for 6 :
10 ripe but still firm tomatoes
2 mild onions
2 pinches of chopped basil leaves
12 chopped tarragon leaves
Olive oil
A dash of wine vinegar
Salt, freshly ground pepper.

Peel and seed the tomatoes, and slice them finely. Place them in a sieve, sprinkle with cooking salt, and leave them to sweat for 15 minutes.

Meanwhile, slice the onions. Prepare the dressing, pouring in a bowl the basil, the tarragon, the vinegar and 8 to 9 tablespoons of olive oil, and some salt and pepper.

After the tomatoes are drained, lay them in a hollow dish, with the onions on top. Pour the dressing over, stir well, and place the salad in the fridge.

The peeled tomatoes give the "salade" a velvety taste. You may also blend in a few thin slices of mozzarella (a soft fermented italian cheese made from bufflone milk) which harmonises very well with raw tomato.

Tomates farcies
Stuffed tomatoes

Wash the tomatoes, divide them into two, widthways, seed them, remove the fleshy pulp with a spoon and put to one side. Sprinkle the tomatoes with salt and leave them to sweat for about 10 minutes. Lay them in a buttered oven dish, ready to be stuffed. Meanwhile, prepare the stuffing as follows.

Brown the minced onion and the tomato flesh in a frying pan with 3 to 4 tablespoons of olive oil for about 5 minutes on a medium heat, add the meat, the garlic, the parsley, the bread or melba toast, soaked in warm milk, the salt and pepper and the herbes de Provence. Stir well, and leave to cook for about 10 minutes. Add the 2 egg yolks, taking care to blend them well with the other ingredients, and check the seasoning.

Fill the tomatoes with the stuffing, sprinkle with a dash of olive oil, and brown it for 25 minutes. You can serve this dish either warm or cold, according to the season.

In the *Vegetables* chapter, you will find five different recipes for vegetables cooked in the same way. You can prepare several kinds of these and serve them with rice. It is colourful and very popular.

Tourte à la ratatouille
Ratatouille pie

Wash the vegetables and peel the courgettes and the aubergines, then cut them into cubes 1.5 cm square. After you have seeded the peppers, cut them into strips. In a frying pan, brown the courgettes first with a few tablespoons of olive oil, until they are brown. Remove them from the frying pan, drain them and put to one side.

Add some more olive oil in the frying pan, fry the aubergines, remove them, drain, and put to one side. Sweat the onions in the same frying pan, add the lardons, and, when they are brown, add the tomato, the garlic and the salt and pepper. Leave to reduce for 10 minutes on a brisk heat. Remove this "coulis" from the pan, and put to one side. Finally, fry the onions, add some salt and pepper, then drain them after they are cooked.

Mix all the ingredients in a large saucepan and check the seasoning.

Butter a pie tin, lay the crust in it, and pour in the vegetable preparation, which you should cover with another layer of pastry. Brush the top layer with an egg yolk, and cook the "tourte" in a hot oven for about 35 minutes.

Serve hot. This dish is originally from Nice.

Eggs, pasta & cheese

Brouillade d'œufs à la truffe
Scrambled eggs and truffle

Preparation time :
10 minutes
Cooking time : 35 minutes

Ingredients for 6 :
12 to 15 eggs
1 fresh truffle or a small can
of truffles peel (in this case,
keep the cooking liquid)
1 teaspoon of Madeira wine
Butter
Olive oil
Salt
Freshly ground pepper.

Clean the truffle with a wet brush, and slice it finely. Put to one side. In a shallow bowl, break the eggs and whisk them carefully, add the fresh truffle or the peel and, in this case, don't forget to add 2 teaspoons of the cooking liquid, and add the Madeira wine. Season with salt and epper.

Rub the bottom of a frying pan with a clove of garlic and then heat up 1 tablespoon of olive oil, and 1 of butter, and pour in the preparation. Quickly scramble the eggs with a fork for about 4 or 5 minutes on a medium heat.

Serve immediately. In order to make the *brouillade* still smoother, you can prepare it in a bain marie. The cooking time will then be 8 minutes.

Crespeou

Preparation time :
60 minutes
Cooking time : 40 minutes

Ingredients for 6 :
18 eggs
1 handful of sorrel, browned
in butter with salt and pepper
1 cup of seasoned coulis de
tomates
1 red pepper, diced and browned with salt and pepper
1/2 cup of cooked spinach and
cream, and a pinch of minced
capers, and some salt and
pepper
1/2 sliced onion browned in
butter with salt and pepper
1 handful of cultivated mushrooms, browned and seasoned
30 g/1 oz of grated cheese
1 tablespoon of minced herbs
(basil, chives, and tarragon).

A *crespéou* is composed of 9 small omelettes placed one on top of another. You should cook, with as little fat as possible and in a non-stick pan, each ome-lette of 2 eggs seasoned with one of the eight prepa-rations mentioned in the opposite column. The ninth should be plain.

As you cook them, place the 9 same-sized ome-lettes on top of the others.

This dish is served hot or cold according to the seasons, with coulis de tomates (see the *sauces* chap-ter). As you cut the cake, you will obtain very colour-ful pieces, thanks to the diversity of the ingredients used.

You can prepare this dish one day beforehand.

Macaronis aux anchois
Macaroni with anchovies

Preparation : 10 minutes
Cooking time : about 10 minutes according to the type of pasta

Ingredients for 6 :
500 g/1 lb of macaroni
8 soaked anchovies
6 tablespoons of coulis de tomates, (see in the *sauces* chapter)
3 tablespoons of olive oil
50 g/2 oz of fresh butter
100 g/4 oz of grated cheese or Parmesan
Salt
Freshly ground pepper.

Sweat the anchovies with one or two tablespoons of olive oil, in a saucepan, and over a slow heat. Add the coulis de tomates, blend it well with the anchovies and leave to cook for 2 or 3 minutes.

Check the seasoning and put to one side.

Meanwhile, throw the macaroni in 2 l of salted boiling water, with a dash of olive oil. As soon as they are cooked, drain them, and add 50 g of butter, which you should blend well with the pasta.

Lay the macaroni in a hollow dish and cover with the tomato and anchovy coulis. Serve the grated cheese or the Parmesan separate.

Nouilles à l'oseille
Noodles and sorrel

Preparation time :
15 minutes
Cooking time : 3 to 6
minutes, according to the
type of noodles

Ingredients for 6 :
500 g/1 lb of fresh noodles
400 g/15 oz of fresh sorrel
Butter
1 bowl of grated cheese, or
Parmesan
1 pinch of ground nutmeg
Salt
Freshly ground pepper.

Clean the sorrel by removing its ribs, wash it abundantly, and drain it. Brown it with 2 tablespoons of butter for 3 or 4 minutes in a saucepan, season with salt and pepper and a pinch of nutmeg. Put to one side.

Meanwhile, throw the noodles in 2 l of salted boiling water with a dash of olive oil. Drain them as soon as they are cooked, and lay them in a dish. Add 50 g of fresh butter and the sorrel purée. Mix well and serve immediately.

You can present it with grated cheese or Parmesan in a separate bowl.

Œufs au coulis de tomates
Eggs and tomato purée

**Preparation time :
15 minutes
Cooking time : 20 minutes**

Ingredients for 6 :
12 eggs
8 big tomatoes, peeled and seeded
1 onion
Basil
Tarragon
Oregano
Thyme
1 bay leaf
Olive oil
1 pinch of sugar
Salt
Freshly ground pepper.

Boil the eggs for 10 minutes shell them and put to one side. Meanwhile, brown the sliced onion with 2 to 3 tablespoons of olive oil in a frying pan and add the tomatoes, the pinch of thyme, the basil, the tarragon, the oregano, the sugar, the salt and the pepper.

Leave this preparation to reduce until it thickens a little and put it through the food processor.

Check the seasoning and blend in the eggs, divided into two lengthwise, with the coulis de tomates.

This dish can be served hot or chilled according to the seasons.

Œufs farcis à l'oseille
Sorrel stuffed eggs

Preparation time :
30 minutes
Cooking time : 20 minutes

Ingredients for 6 :
9 eggs
600 g/1,3 lb of fresh sorrel
2 crushed cloves of garlic
2 pinches of minced parsley
2 slices of sandwich bread
1 cup of crumbs
1 dl of milk
Oil
Butter
Salt
Freshly ground pepper.

Boil the eggs for 10 minutes, shell and cut into two, lengthwise. Put to one side. Meanwhile, clean the sorrel by removing its ribs, wash it abundantly and drain it. Brown it with 2 tablespoons of butter, the garlic, the parsley, the salt and the pepper for 3 or 4 minutes. Put to one side.

Soak the bread in the warm milk and, when it has softened, break it into a "pommade" with a fork, and put to one side. Take the boiled egg yolks and mash them in a hollow dish with 4 to 5 tablespoons of olive oil. Add the sorrel and the bread, and mix well. Check the seasoning. This is the stuffing which you will use to fill the boiled egg whites, which you should lay on an oven dish.

Sprinkle a pinch of crumbs over each egg, as well as a very small knob of butter. Pour 3 tablespoons of water as well as a few knobs of butter in the bottom of the dish and cook the eggs au gratin in a medium oven for 20 minutes.

This dish can be served hot or warmed according to the season. In this chapter, you will find 3 successive but different recipes for stuffed eggs that you might want to cook at the same time. It then constitutes a colourful and variegated dish.

Œufs farcis à la provençale
Stuffed eggs a la Provencal

Preparation time :
40 minutes
Cooking time : 20 minutes

Ingredients for 6 :
9 eggs
7 to 8 ripe tomatoes, peeled and seeded
1 onion
2 slices of sandwich bread
200 g/7 oz of minced meat
1 pinch of sugar
2 tablespoons of olive oil
20 g/1 oz of butter
Basil
Tarragon
Salt
Freshly ground pepper.

Boil the eggs for 10 minutes, shell them and cut them into two, lengthwise. Put to one side. Meanwhile, brown the minced onion and the tomatoes with a little oil and butter. Leave the tomato purée to reduce for about 10 minutes, and put it to one side.

Soak the sandwich bread in the milk. When it has softened, break it into a *pommade* with a fork, and put it as well to one side. Take the boiled eggs yolks and mash them in a hollow dish with 6 to 7 tablespoons of olive oil, before putting it to one side.

Cook the minced meat in a non-stick pan for 5 to 6 minutes, and add the coulis de tomates, the white part of the bread (called "mic de pain" in France), and the egg yolks. Mix these ingredients well, and check the seasoning. This constitutes the stuffing you will use to fill the boiled egg whites, which you should lay on an oven dish.

Pour 3 tablespoons of water and 4 to 5 knobs of butter in the bottom of the dish and cook the eggs au gratin in a medium oven for 20 minutes. This dish can be served hot or warm according to the season. In this chapter, you will find 3 successive but different recipes for stuffed eggs that you might want to cook at the same time. It then constitutes a colourful and variegated dish.

Œufs farcis aux épinards
Spinach stuffed spinach

Preparation time :
45 minutes
Cooking time : 20 minutes

Ingredients for 6 :
9 eggs
1 onion
2 tomatoes
500 g/1 lb of spinach
1 teaspoon of capers
2 pinches of minced parsley
1 pinch of ground nutmeg
Butter
Olive oil
Salt
Freshly ground pepper.

Boil the eggs for 10 minutes, shell them, and cut them into two, lengthwise. Put to one side. While the eggs are cooking, brown the minced onion with one tablespoon of olive oil and one teaspoon of butter for about 3 to 4 minutes. Add the tomatoes, leave to reduce for a quarter of an hour, and put to one side.

Clean the spinach, blanch them in a saucepan filled with salted boiling water for 10 minutes. Drain and then sweat them in a frying pan with a tablespoon of butter, and add the parsley, the chopped capers, and a pinch of ground nutmeg. Take the boiled egg yolks and mash them in a hollow dish with a few tablespoons of olive oil until it forms a "pommade". Then, add the tomato purée and the spinach preparation, and blend all the ingredients. Check the seasoning. This *pommade* constitutes the stuffing which you will use to fill the boiled egg whites, which you should lay on an oven dish.

Pour 3 tablespoons of water as well as a few knobs of butter in the bottom of the dish and cook the eggs au gratin in a medium oven for 20 minutes. The eggs can be served hot or warm. In this chapter, you will find 3 successive but different recipes for stuffed eggs that you might want to cook at the same time. It then constitutes a colourful and variegated dish.

Œufs gratinés à la provençale
Eggs au gratin a la Provencal

Preparation time :
15 minutes
Cooking time : 10 minutes

Ingredients for 6 :
9 eggs
1 clove of garlic
1 onion
50 g/2 oz of butter
2 tablespoons of flour
1/4 l/1/2 Pt of milk
2 teaspoons of crème fraîche
or double cream
1 pinch of ground nutmeg
1 cup of parmesan or grated
cheese
Salt
Freshly ground pepper.

Boil the eggs for 10 minutes, shell them, and cut them into two, lengthwise. Put to one side. In a saucepan, brown the sliced onion, and the crushed garlic clove with 50 g of butter, until they are browned.

Add the flour, stir well, and pour little by little, stirring continuously 1/4 l of milk, until the sauce thickens. Season with salt and pepper, and add the ground nutmeg and the cream.

Butter an oven dish, lay the hard-boiled eggs inside and cover them with sauce. Sprinkle with grated cheese and a few knobs of butter, and brown in a medium oven for about 10 minutes.

Œufs pochés à la crème de champignons

Poached eggs with mushroom cream

Preparation time :
25 minutes
Cooking time : 3 minutes

Ingredients for 6 :
12 eggs
4 to 5 tablespoons of wine vinegar
1/2 l/1 Pt of water
5 to 6 twigs of parsley
Salt
Freshly ground pepper
1 bowl of mushroom cream
(see this recipe in the *sauces* chapter).

Prepare the cream according to the recipe in the *sauces* chapter, and maintain it warm. Pour the water and the vinegar in a small saucepan and delicately slide the eggs in it and poach them for 3 minutes.

Remove and drain.

Lay the eggs in small dishes, season them with salt and pepper, top them with a tablespoon of mushroom cream, and sprinkle with minced parsley.

Serve immediately.

Omelette à l'ail et aux fines herbes
Garlic and herbs omelette

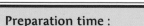

Preparation time :
5 minutes
Cooking time : 5 minutes

Ingredients for 6 :
12 eggs
2 peeled garlic cloves
5 twigs of parsley
10 twigs of fresh chives
2 tablespoons of crème fraîche or double cream
20 g/1 oz of butter
2 tablespoons of olive oil
Salt
Freshly ground pepper.

Finely mince the garlic, the parsley, and the chives. Break and whisk the eggs in a hollow dish, and blend in the minced herbs and garlic, the cream, and the salt and pepper.

Heat the butter and the oil in a frying pan, and when it is hot, delicately pour in the whisked eggs, and leave them to cook for 4 to 5 minutes on a brisk heat. The omelette shouldn't be too cooked, as it has to be runny to stay smooth.

Roll the omelette on a warmed dish and serve immediately.

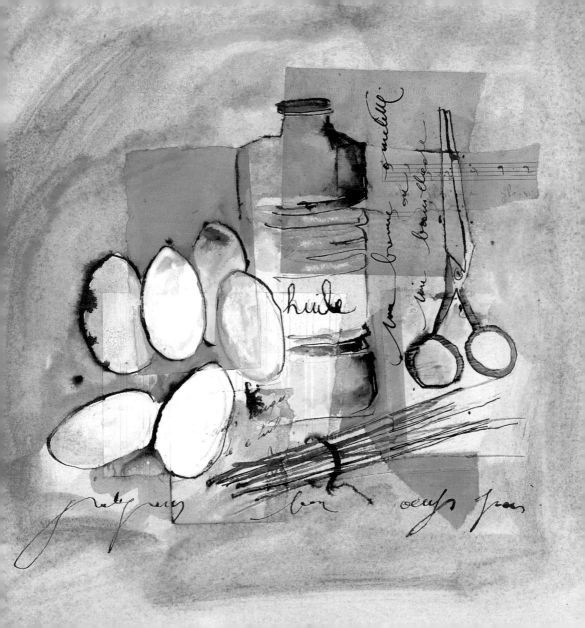

Omelette à la tomate
Tomato omelette

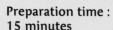

**Preparation time :
15 minutes
Cooking time : 5 minutes**

Ingredients for 6 :
12 eggs
3 peeled and seeded tomatoes
1 onion
1 tablespoon of crème fraîche
or double cream
4 to 5 basil leaves
Olive oil
Salt
Freshly ground pepper.

Brown the minced onion in 2 tablespoons of olive oil in a frying pan for 3 to 4 minutes, add the chopped tomatoes, the salt, the pepper, and the basil. Leave the preparation to reduce, and put to one side.

Break and whisk the eggs in a hollow dish and blend in the tomato purée and the cream. Check the seasoning.

In a frying pan, heat 20 g of butter and a tablespoon of olive oil, and when the mixture is hot, pour delicately the omelette in, and cook it for 4 to 5 minutes on a brisk heat, stirring continuously. It shouldn't be too cooked as it has to stay runny to be smooth.

Roll the omelette on a warmed dish and serve immediately.

Omelette aux asperges
Asparagus omelette

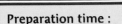

Preparation time :
5 minutes
Cooking time : 5 minutes

Ingredients for 6 :
12 eggs
12 cooked points of green asparagus
20 g / 1 oz of grated cheese
2 tablespoons of crème fraîche or double cream
Butter
Peanut oil
Salt
Freshly ground pepper.

Brown the points of asparagus with 30 g of butter for 2 to 3 minutes on a medium heat. Season with salt and pepper, and put to one side.

Break and whisk the eggs in a hollow dish, and add the cream, the grated cheese as well as a little salt and pepper.

Heat 1 tablespoon of olive oil and 20 g of butter in a frying pan, and when this mixture is hot, pour in the whisked eggs. Add the asparagus points only when the omelette is half-cooked so that they don't break too much.

Cook the omelette for 4 to 5 minutes on a brisk heat, but it should stay runny and smooth however.

Roll the omelette on a warm dish and serve immediately.

Pâtes au basilic

Pesto pasta

Preparation time :
5 minutes
Cooking time :
4 to 5 minutes

Ingredients for 6 :
500 g/1 lb of fresh pasta
2 garlic cloves
4 to 5 fresh basil leaves
Olive oil
Salt, freshly ground pepper.

Put the peeled garlic, the basil leaves and 6 to 7 tablespoons of olive oil, salt, and pepper in the food processor, and blend. Put to one side.

Throw the pasta in a large saucepan filled with salted boiling water and a dash of olive oil. Cook for 4 to 5 minutes (according to the type of pasta) after the first boil.

Drain, then pour them quickly in a hollow dish with the pesto sauce.

Serve the Parmesan cheese separately.

You can put in more or less garlic according to your taste, when you prepare the pesto sauce. Don't forget that raw garlic is much stronger than cooked garlic and white garlic is milder than purple garlic. It is up to you.

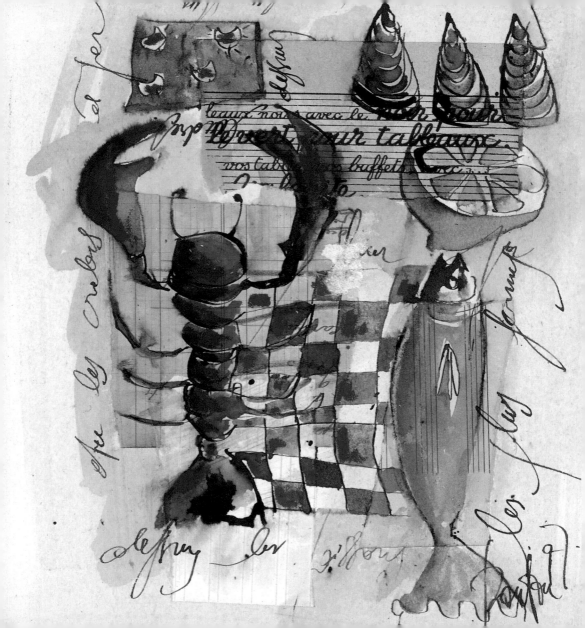

Fish & seafood

Aiguillettes de dorade et de loup au basilic

Gilt-head and bass aiguillettes with basil

Preparation time :
10 minutes
Cooking time : 7 minutes

Ingredients for 6 :
500 g/1 lb of bass fillets
500 g/1 lb of gilt-head fillets
1 lemon
15 fresh basil leaves
1 shallot
Olive oil
Salt
Freshly ground pepper.

Cook all of the fish fillets for 5 minutes in a micro-wave or for 6 to 7 minutes in court bouillon after the first boil. Drain the fish well.

Cut the fish in aiguillettes and lay the pieces in a hollow dish.

Squeeze the lemon juice, pour it in a bowl with a pinch of salt and pepper, as well as the minced basil and shallot, and about 1 dl of olive oil. Blend well, and pour this sauce over the fish. Stir delicately, check the seasoning and serve chilled.

You can make this salad with other varieties of fish (monkfish, salmon, etc.). It is also possible to add a few pieces of salmon cut into strips so as to give a slightly different flavour to this salad.

Brandade de morue
Cod brandade

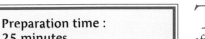

Preparation time :
25 minutes
Cooking time :
about 15 minutes

Ingredients for 6 :
1 kg/2 lb of soaked cod (failing
that, soak the cod in 2 of
fresh water for 24 hours,
changing it 2 or 3 times),
3 dl/1/2 Pt of olive oil
1 dl/1/4 Pt of milk
1 dl/1/4 Pt of crème fraîche
or double cream
1 lemon juice
1 pinch of ground nutmeg
1 pinch of ground thyme
1 bay leaf
24 cubes of sandwich bread
Freshly ground pepper.

Throw the cod in 2 l of fresh cold water, with the thyme, and the bay leaf, and cook it for 8 minutes after the first boil. Remove the saucepan from the heat and leave the fish for 5 more minutes in the saucepan.

Drain the cod, and remove the skin and bones. Crumble the flesh, pound it, and place it in a casserole rubbed with a crushed garlic clove.

Slightly heat the milk and the cream in a saucepan, and the oil in another.

Work the cod energetically on a very low heat with a wooden spoon, incorporating alternatively small quantities of oil and milk, until the cod looks like a thick cream. Add a dash of lemon juice, and pour in freshly ground pepper.

If the brandade is not thick enough, you can incorporate 2 or 3 tablespoons of well seasoned and thick "béchamel" sauce.

The *brandade* can be served either hot with fried croûtons, or cold with a salad of crudités.

Encornets à la provençale
Squids a la Provencal

**Preparation time :
10 minutes
Cooking time : 30 minutes**

Ingredients for 6 :
1.5 kg/3 lb of squids
4 ripe tomatoes
2 onions
3 garlic cloves
80 g/2,5 oz of stoned black olives
2 pinches of minced parsley
1 bay leaf
1.5 dl/0,3 Pt of dry white wine
2 tablespoons of crème fraîche or double cream
Salt
Freshly ground pepper.

After you have minced the garlic and the onions, sweat them in 3 to 4 tablespoons of olive oil and brown the squids in this same frying pan for 7 to 8 minutes.

Add the peeled and seeded tomatoes, 1 pinch of parsley, a little saffron, the bay leaf, and the salt and pepper. Pour the white wine in, and leave to cook uncovered for 30 minutes on a slow heat.

Five minutes before the end of the cooking time, add the cream, check the seasoning, and serve this hot dish sprinkled with fresh minced parsley.

You can accompany the squids a la Provencal with buttered semolina.

Escabèche de sardines

**Preparation time :
30 minutes
Cooking time : 20 minutes**

Ingredients for 6 :
1 kg/2 lb of sardines
3 carrots
2 onions
1 shallot
2 garlic cloves
4 twigs of parsley
3 bay leaves
1 twig of thyme
2 cloves
1 pinch of ground nutmeg
1 pinch of Cayenne pepper
1 d l of dry white wine
3 dl of wine vinegar
1 dl of water
Olive oil
Salt
Freshly ground pepper.

Wash the sardines, gut them, and remove their heads and dorsal bone by splitting them lengthwise. Lay them in an oven dish or a tureen, and season them slightly with salt and pepper.

Peel and clean the vegetables, and slice them finely. Brown them in a saucepan with 8 to 10 tablespoons of olive oil, season with salt and add all the seasonings mentioned opposite.

When the vegetables are slightly browned, pour in the white wine, the water and the vinegar and boil the whole for 10 minutes.

Pour this boiling marinade over the sardines and put it in the oven for 20 minutes.

This dish is usually served cold, and it is advisable to prepare it one day beforehand. Sprinkle with a dash of olive oil before eating it.

Feuilletés à la morue

Cod pastry

Preparation time :
40 minutes
Cooking time : 30 minutes

Ingredients for 6 :
500 g/1 lb of soaked cod, (failing that, soak it yourself in 2 l of fresh water for 24 hours changing it 2 or 3 times.)
400 g/0,8 lb of puff pastry
1 kg/2 lb of spinach
2 pinches of minced parsley
1 crushed clove of garlic
2 egg yolks
2 whole eggs
3 tablespoons of crème fraîche or double cream
1 pinch of ground nutmeg
1 point of Cayenne pepper
Freshly ground pepper.

After you have washed the spinach, blanch the leaves in 2 l of salted boiling water for 6 or 7 minutes. Rinse them in cold water and drain and chop them.

Throw the cod in cold water, and cook it for 8 minutes past the first boil. Remove the skin and the bones, and crumble the flesh.

In a bowl, mix the spinach, the cod, the cream, the 2 whole eggs, the ground nutmeg, the Cayenne pepper, and the freshly ground pepper, and check the seasoning.

Roll the pastry on a 1/2 cm layer. Cut 6 same sized rectangles (8 cm by 6 cm). Lay the stuffing in their middle, and form the turnovers. Brush the top with egg yolk, and place them on a baking tray. Cook in the oven for about 25 minutes.

This pastry is served hot as a starter, or as a main course. You can top it with saffron sauce, the recipe of which you will find in the *sauces* chapter.

Gambas flambées au pastis
Flambé gambas with pastis

Preparation time :
25 minutes
Cooking time :
about 10 minutes

Ingredients for 6 :
30 middle sized gambas
About 100 g/3,5 oz of crème
fraîche or double cream
2 shallots
A few leaves of fresh tarragon
1 tablespoon of pastis
0.5 dl/0,1 Pt of cognac
Peanut oil
Butter
Salt
Freshly ground pepper.

Shell the raw gambas, throw away their heads and put them to one side. Sweat the shallots in a frying pan over a slow heat with 20 g of butter and 2 tablespoons of olive oil. Throw in the gambas and brown them for 2 minutes on each side.

Season with salt and pepper. Then, pour in the warmed cognac and pastis on the gambas and flambé them for a few seconds on a brisk heat.

Bring the heat down and incorporate the cream in the pan, as well as 2 pinches of fresh minced tarragon. Leave to simmer for 5 minutes and check the seasoning. The subtlety of this dish is linked with the presence of pastis which enhances the tarragon, while keeping in the same range of aromas.

Gâteaux de moules à la menthe fraîche
Mussels cakes with fresh mint

⊃•‹›⊃›⊃⊃))⊃)⊂⊂⊂⊂‹•⊂

Preparation time :
45 minutes
Cooking time : 40 minutes

Ingredients for 6 :
2 1/4 Pt of mussels
1 shallot
1.5 dl/0,3 Pt of dry white wine
2 pinches of thyme flowers
3 egg yolks
3 whole eggs
200 to 250 g of crème fraîche
or double cream
Butter
25 g of grated cheese
4 to 5 twigs of fresh mint
Salt
Freshly ground pepper.

Clean the mussels and open them in a large covered pan with the wine, the minced shallot and 1 pinch of thyme. Stir from time to time, and leave to cook for 10 minutes. Remove the mussels, and remove their shells after they have cooled down. Sieve the cooking liquid through a square of muslin so as to filter any sand which might have stayed in the shells. Put to one side. Blend the 6 egg yolks with 6 tablespoons of cream, the grated cheese, a pinch of freshly ground pepper and a pinch of salt in a food processor. Butter 6 ramekins, lay in each of them a small handful of mussels, and fill them 3/4 full with the egg preparation. Cook the cakes in a bain marie for 40 minutes in an oven (lay the ramekins in an oven dish in which you should pour 1/2 l of water so that the bottom of the ramekins soaks in water. Check whether the gâteaux are cooked by dipping the point of a knife in the cakes. It should come out clean if the cakes are cooked.

Prepare the mint sauce by pouring the mussels cooking juice in a small saucepan, add the chopped fresh leaves of mint as well as a tablespoon of cream and a little freshly ground pepper. Boil for 2 to 3 minutes and incorporate with a whisk, away from the fire, 50 g of butter. Check the seasoning (be careful with salt, as the mussels cooking juice is already salty) and turn out the cakes. Top them with the warm sauce.

Gratin de la Méditerranée
Mediterranean gratin

Preparation time : 45 mn
Cooking time : 10 mn

Ingredients for 6 :
500 g//1 lb of fillets of bass
500 g/1 lb of fillets
of gilt-head
12 gambas or big
Mediterranean prawn
2 crayfish (optional)
1 carrot
1 onion
1.5 dl/0,3 Pt of dry white wine
Olive oil
Butter

For the sauce :
2 to 3 tablespoons of flour
1/4 l/1/2 Pt of stock (the crayfish cooking juice)
100 g/3,5 Pt of crème fraîche
or double cream
1 pinch of Cayenne pepper
1 pinch of ground nutmeg
30 to 40 g/1 to 1,5 oz of grated cheese
Salt
Freshly ground pepper.

Cut the fish in aiguillettes, shell the shellfish and remove the heads, slice the crayfish, but not the gambas.
Roughly blend the heads through the food processor and
brown in a saucepan with 3 to 4 tablespoons of olive oil, a
minced onion and a minced carrot for 3 to 4 minutes.

Cover with 1/2 to 3/4 l of water as well as with the
white wine. Sieve the cooking liquid (about 1/4 l) and put
to one side.

Meanwhile, melt 50 g of butter in a saucepan, add the
flour, stir well and then pour in the shellfish cooking liquid
progressively and whisk until the sauce thickens. Then, add
the cream, the Cayenne pepper and the ground nutmeg.
Check the seasoning and, away from the heat, incorporate
the grated cheese with a whisk.

In a frying pan, brown the fish aiguillettes, the crayfish
medaillons, and the gambas in 50 g of butter and a tablespoon of olive oil for 3 or 4 minutes. Season with salt and
pepper.

Butter an oven dish, lay the fish in and cover them with
the sauce. Brown in the oven for 5 minutes.

This gratin should be served very hot and can be served
with a *flan d'épinards*.

Lotte à la fondue de tomates
Monkfish with tomato purée

Preparation time :
25 minutes
Cooking time : 10 minutes

Ingredients for 6 :
1.5 kg/3 lb of fillet
 of monkfish
1.5 kg/3 lb of ripe tomatoes
10 leaves of fresh tarragon
1 pinch of thyme flowers
1 pinch of Cayenne pepper
Olive oil
Butter
Salt
Freshly ground pepper.

Peel and seed the tomatoes, chop and brown them with 5 to 6 tablespoons of olive oil in a frying pan. Add a pinch of thyme, the minced tarragon, and the salt and pepper. Leave to cook for about 10 minutes. Check the seasoning and put to one side.

Prepare 6 buttered squares of tin foil, place about 1 teaspoon of tomato purée in each of them, lay a piece of fish seasoned with salt and pepper and top with another teaspoon of tomato purée.

Close tightly and cook on a baking tray in a hot oven for 8 to 10 minutes. Serve very hot.

The fish should be quickly taken out of the foil and topped with the rest of tomato purée, which you should have blended with a knob of fresh butter and a pinch of sugar. Check the seasoning.

Poêlée de coquilles Saint-Jacques à l'estragon

Scallops and tarrragon

Preparation time :
15 minutes
Cooking time : 3 minutes

Ingredients for 6 :
30 scallops
4 shallots,
12 minced leaves of tarragon
1 dl of crème fraîche or
double cream
4 tablespoons of fine
Champagne
2 tablespoons of port wine
Butter
Salt
Freshly ground pepper.

Peel the shallots and mince them. Sweat them slowly in a frying pan with 30 g of butter for 4 to 5 minutes. Add the scallops and brown them for about 3 minutes, stirring constantly. Season with salt and pepper and flambé with the pre-heated fine champagne. Remove the scallops with a skimmer and put to one side.

Deglaze the scallops cooking juice with the cream and 2 tablespoons of port wine, add the tarragon and leave to cook for 2 to 3 minutes. Blend the sauce and 50 g of fresh butter through the food processor.

Check the seasoning and top the scallops with this sauce and sprinkle with a few tarragon leaves. This dish has a subtle taste and you can serve it with a pumpkin flan or a tomato soufflé.

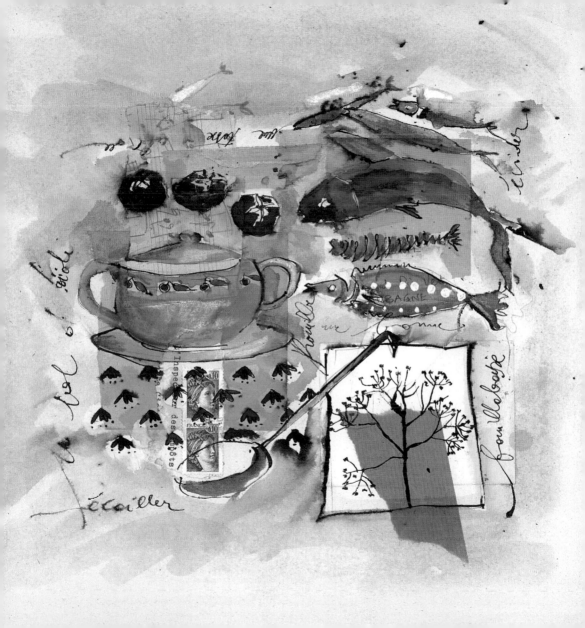

Poisson cru mariné aux herbes de Provence

Marinated raw fish with herbes de Provence

Preparation time :
40 minutes
Cooking time : no cooking,
but the fish must however
be marinated for at least
6 hours.

Ingredients for 6 :
450 g/1 lb of fillets of salmon
450 g/1 lb of fillets of gilt-head
4 middle sized lemon
5 shallots
2 pinches of freshly minced chives, tarragon and basil
1.5 dl/0,3 Pt of olive oil
Salt
Freshly ground pepper.

Cut the fillets in small and fine strips, as thick as a slice of smoked salmon. Lay the fish in a hollow dish, and put to one side.

Peel the shallots and mince them finely.

Squeeze the lemon juice, pour it in a bowl with 1 pinch of salt, 3 or 4 pinches of freshly ground pepper, the aromatic herbs, the shallots and the olive oil.

Pour the marinade over the fish so that it soaks. Place the dish in a fridge for about 6 hours. Give the preparation a stir every 2 or 3 hours so that all the pieces are soaked in the marinade. The lemon juice should whiten the fish, "cooking" the flesh at the same time.

This salad has to be served chilled and makes a perfect starter in every season. You can use any other variety of saltwater fish (monkfish, grouper, mullet, etc.) to prepare this salad.

Rougets à la mode provençale
Mullet a la Provencal

Take off the fillets, keeping the skin, and remove the bones with tweezers. Season with salt and pepper and put to one side.

In a saucepan, brown the bones and the heads with 4 to 5 tablespoons of olive oil and a few peppercorns. Fill the saucepan with water and add the white wine and the parsley.

Cook for 20 minutes, and sieve this stock.

Then, brown the garlic and the onions with 25 g of butter, and add the stock and a dash of vinegar. Leave to reduce for about 10 minutes and away from the fire, whisk in 50 g of butter. Check the seasoning and put to one side.

In a non-stick pan, brown on a brisk heat the fillets on the side of their skin for 2 to 3 minutes, and turn them over for another minute. Lay them in a hollow dish, top them with sauce, and serve immediately.

This dish can be served either chilled or hot according to the seasons.

Preparation time :
45 minutes
Cooking time : 5 minutes

Ingredients for 6 :
6 mullets
(about 200 g/0,5 lb each)
1 onion
1 garlic clove
1.5 dl/0,3 Pt of dry white wine
4 twigs of parsley
A dash of white wine vinegar
A twig of fennel
Olive oil
Salt
Freshly ground pepper
Peppercorns.

Salade de moules à la ciboulette
Mergels salad with chives

Mussels salad with chives

Preparation time :
25 minutes
Cooking time : 10 minutes

Ingredients for 6 :
3 kg / 6 lb of mussels
1 onion
1 dl / 1/4 Pt of dry white wine
1 pinch of ground thyme
5 to 6 tablespoons of mayonnaise, to which you should add
a pinch of Cayenne pepper
and 3 drops of tabasco
1.5 dl / 0.3 pt of the mussels
cooking juice
15 twigs of chives, minced
Salt
Freshly ground pepper.

Clean the mussels and open them on a brisk heat in a large covered saucepan, with the white wine, the minced onion, and the thyme for about 10 minutes stirring from time to time.

Remove the mussels from the saucepan with a skimmer and leave them to cool down. Take 1,5 dl of the cooking juice and sieve it through a square of muslin so as to filter any sand which might have stayed in the shells.

In a bowl, mix the mayonnaise, the cooking juice and the chives. Pour this sauce over the mussels and place the salad in the fridge.

This dish should be served chilled.

Salade de supions à l'ail et au citron

Cuttlefish salad with garlic and lemon

Preparation time :
7 or 8 minutes
Cooking time : 5 minutes

Ingredients for 6 :
1.2 kg/2,5 lb of small and tender cuttlefish, washed well
2 pinches of minced parsley
2 twigs of tarragon
1 twig of fennel
2 crushed cloves of garlic
1 lemon
0.5 to 1 dl/0,1 to 0,2 Pt of olive oil
Salt
Freshly ground pepper.

Cook the cuttlefish in a saucepan filled with salted water for 4 to 5 minutes from its first boil. Drain and lay in a hollow dish.

Squeeze the juice of a lemon, pour it in a bowl with the parsley, the minced tarragon, garlic, and fennel, and the olive oil, and the salt and pepper. Blend well, pour this sauce over the cuttlefish, stir, and serve chilled.

This salad constitutes a popular and easy to prepare starter. You can add a few dice of raw tomato, which accompany well the cuttlefish and add a nice touch of colour to this salad.

Saumon fumé chaud aux herbes de Provence

Warm smoked salmon with herbes de Provence

Preparation time :
15 minutes
Cooking time : 2 minutes

Ingredients for 6 :
1 to 2 slices of smoked salmon
for each guest
1 pinch of fresh basil, tarragon
and chives
250 g/8 oz of crème fraîche or
double cream
A small jar of salmon roe
Freshly ground pepper.

Finely mince the basil, the tarragon, and the chives. Add the cream and 3 to 4 pinches of pepper. Don't season with salt as the salmon will naturally salt the marinade.

A quarter of an hour before cooking the salmon, lay the slices in a hollow dish, and cover them with the mixture of cream and herbs so that they soak.

Heat a large non-stick frying pan and brown the slices of salmon still impregnated with the cream for 1 minute on each side (they should withdraw when heated). Check the seasoning and lay them on the plates. Top with a little roe and a pinch of aromatic herbs.

This dish can be served hot as a starter or if you count 2 slices of salmon per guest, as a main course. It can then be served with spinach as a side dish.

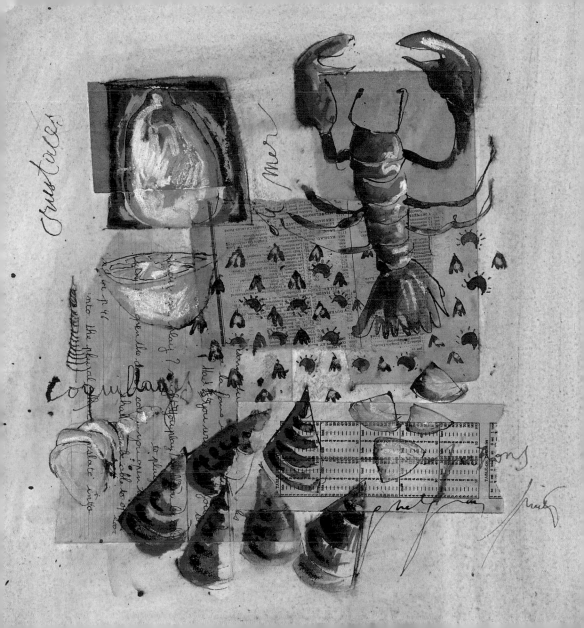

Terrine de lotte à la tomate
Monkfish and tomato pâté

Preparation time : 25 minutes
Cooking time : 30 minutes

Ingredients for 6 :
600 to 700 g//1,3 to 1,5 lb of cleaned monkfish
1 kg/2 lb of ripe tomatoes
6 eggs
1 onion
1 clove of garlic
7 or 8 fresh leaves of basil
A few leaves of fresh basil
1 pinch of thyme flowers
1 pinch of caster sugar
Olive oil
Salt
Freshly ground pepper.

Cut the monkfish into large pieces, cook it for 4 minutes in a microwave or 5 minutes past the first boil in a saucepan filled with salted and peppered water. Drain, and put to one side. Brown it in 5 or 6 tablespoons of olive oil, the minced onion, the crushed garlic, the peeled and seeded tomatoes, and add the herbs (thyme, basil, tarragon) and the salt and pepper, as well as a pinch of caster sugar. Leave this coulis to reduce for about 10 minutes on a medium heat.

Whisk the eggs to which you should add the tomatoes, and then the monkfish. Check the seasoning.

Butter a tureen or a tin and pour in the preparation. Cook for 30 minutes in a preheated oven au bain marie. Check whether the cake is cooked by dipping the point of a knife in it. The knife should come out clean.

Leave the cake to cool down and slice it with an electric knife if possible, so as to obtain neat slices.

This dish can be prepared one day beforehand. It has to be served chilled, and can be presented with a mayonnaise or a "sauce aux fines herbes" (you can find this recipe in the *sauce* chapter).

Meats
&
poultry

Andouillettes braisées à l'Espérandieu

Preparation time :
10 minutes
Cooking time : 45 minutes

Ingredients for 6 :
6 pure pork "andouillettes"
(small sausages made of chit-
terlings)
4 shallots
3 pinches of minced parsley
Ideally 1/2 l of Côtes du Rhône
rosé Espérandieu (or any
other rosé wine)
Salt
Freshly ground pepper.

Peel the shallots and mince them with parsley. Put to one side. Prick the *andouillettes* with a fork and lay them in an oven dish (a clay dish if possible). Sprinkle with the shallots and the parsley and pour in the wine so that the *andouillettes* soak. Season with salt and pepper, and cover with tin foil.

Cook it in a hot oven for about 45 minutes. The mine should be absorbed by the *andouillettes* and the shallots.

This dish is tasty and is not in the least difficult to prepare. You can serve a "purée de pommes de terre" as a side dish.

You should always chose high quality *andouillettes*. So that they cook better, take them out of the fridge at least 2 hours before cooking them. Remove them carefully from the dish with a spatula.

Blancs de poulets à l'estragon
Chicken breasts with tarragon

Preparation time :
20 minutes
Cooking time : 40 minutes

Ingredients for 6 :
6 chicken breasts
400 g/0,8 lb of cultivated
mushrooms or other varieties
such as ceps, chanterelles, or
morels (in this case, one handful should be enough to flavour the dish), cleaned
1 big onion
1/4 l/1/2 Pt of white wine
300 g/10 oz of crème fraîche
or double cream
15 fresh leaves of tarragon
1 small pinch of ground nutmeg
1 tablespoon of cornflour/
cornstarch
Salt
Freshly ground pepper.

Peel the onion, mince it as well as the mushrooms and brown them in a frying pan with 3 tablespoons of olive oil and 25 g of butter for 5 or 6 minutes. Season with salt and pepper, and put to one side.

Blend in the food processor the cream, the white wine, the salt, the pepper and the ground nutmeg.

Season each side of the breasts with salt and pepper. Butter an oven dish and lay the breasts first, then the browned mushrooms and onion. Pour the preparation made with cream in, sprinkle with the minced leaves of tarragon, and cook in a hot oven for 35 to 40 minutes.

Remove the breasts and the mushrooms from the oven and keep them warm. Pour the cooking liquid in a saucepan, and heat it up. With a whisk, incorporate 1 tablespoon of cornflour mixed in one tablespoon of water. Cook for 2 to 3 minutes until the sauce thickens and blend it in a food processor. Check the seasoning.

Serve the breasts topped with the sauce sprinkled with fresh tarragon, and with fresh pasta as a side dish. If you have enough time, marinade the breasts in the cream for 2 to 3 hours before cooking them, as they will be smoother.

Bœuf aux anchois
Beef and anchovies

**Preparation time :
25 minutes
Cooking time : 2 h 15**

Ingredients for 6 :
2 kg/4 lb of rump steak
8 salted anchovies
1 onion
150 g/ 5 oz of capers
5 to 6 gherkins
2 cloves
8 cloves of garlic
1 bouquet garni
1 dl/1/4 Pt of cognac
1 bottle of red wine Côtes du Rhônes
Olive oil
Salt
Freshly ground pepper.

Mince the soaked anchovies, the capers and the gherkins together and put to one side. Brown the minced onions in a saucepan with 3 to 4 tablespoons of olive oil, add the meat cut into big dice, season with salt and pepper, and brown for about 10 minutes. Pour in the cognac, flambé the meat and add the bouquet garni, the cloves, the crushed garlic and the wine.

Bring to the boil for 5 minutes and place the meat in an oven casserole. Close it tightly and leave to cook for about 2 hours in the oven, on a slow heat.

Twenty minutes before the end of the cooking time, add the minced anchovies, gherkins and capers in the casserole. Check the seasoning before serving. You can mix the sauce in the food processor if you want.

This dish can be served with big macaroni as a side dish. You can prepare the beef and anchovies one day beforehand, it will only taste better if it is reheated. Take the meat out of the fridge 2 to 3 hours before cooking it.

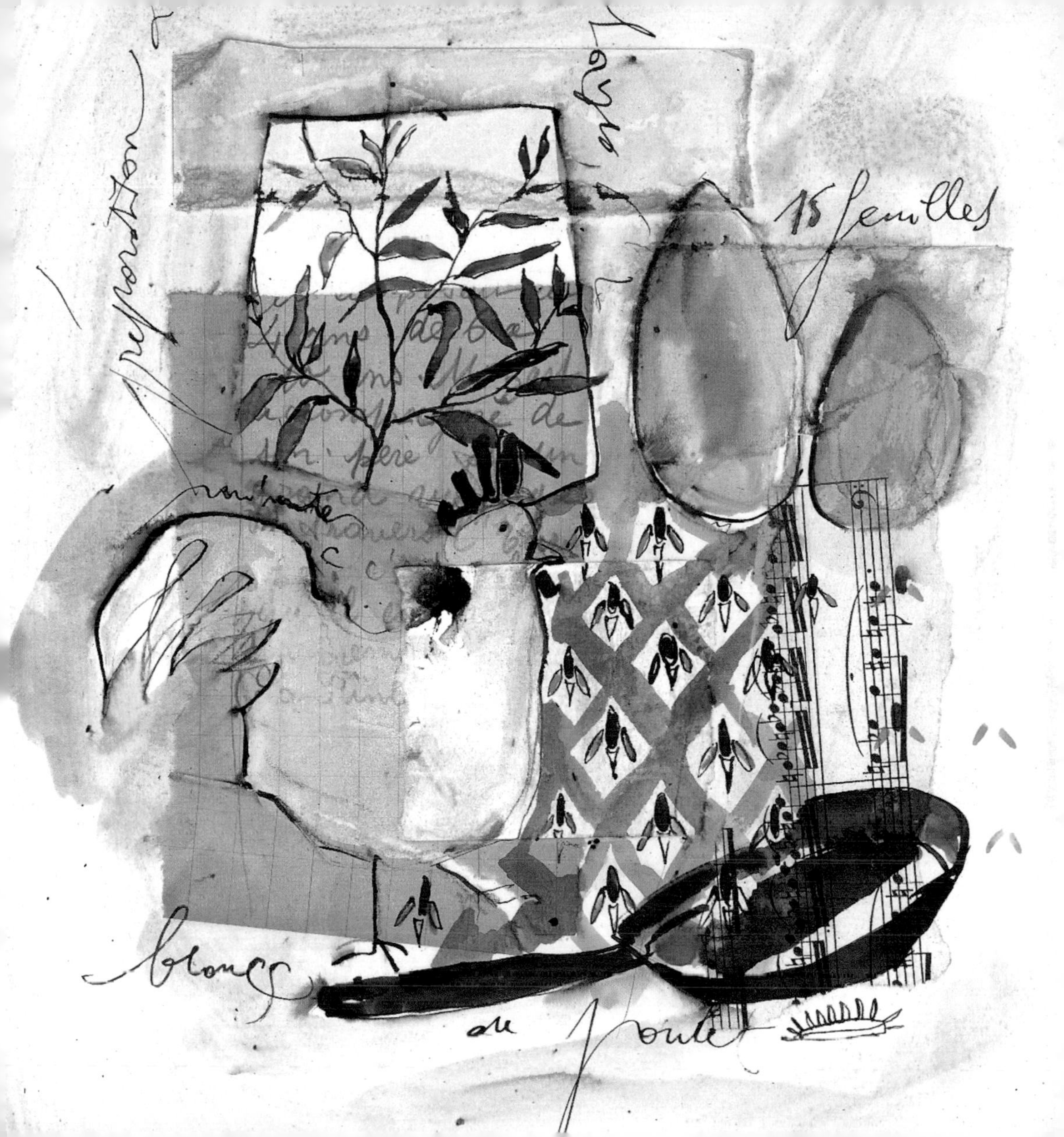

préparation
15 feuilles
blancs

Caillettes provençales

**Preparation time :
30 minutes
Cooking time : 40 minutes**

Ingredients for 6 :
150 g/5 oz of pork liver
200 g/7 oz of pork chine
1 onion
3 garlic clove
Parsley
Chervil
Chives
2 juniper berries
Ground nutmeg
500 g/1 lb of spinach
3 eggs
1 piece of caul
1 glass of dry white wine
100 g/3,5 oz of lard
Salt
Freshly ground pepper.

Blanch the spinach for 5 minutes in salted boiling water. Drain well, mince finely and put to one side. Mince the meat with the garlic, the onion, 3 to 4 twigs of parsley, a pinch of chervil, half a bunch of chives, the juniper berries, a pinch of ground nutmeg, some salt and pepper.

In a hollow dish, blend now the spinach with the minced meat, add the beaten eggs, and check the seasoning.

Cut the caul with scissors into 6 to 8 parts (according to how big you want the *caillettes*), share the stuffing into 6 or 8 parts which you will wrap in the ...

Butter an oven dish, lay the *caillettes* in it, add 2 tablespoons of lard as well as the white wine and leave to cook for about 40 minutes. Baste from time to time with the cooking liquid.

The *caillettes* can be served warm or cold. Slice them finely and serve it with curly endive.

Charlotte d'agneau aux aubergines

lamb and aubergines charlotte

Preparation time :
55 minutes
Cooking time : 25 minutes

Ingredients for 6 :
1.5 kg/3 lb of aubergines/ egg-plants
600 g/1,3 lb of boned shoulder of lamb
1 handful of rice
5 eggs
About ten fresh leaves of mint
1 pinch of cumin
2 pinches of Cayenne pepper
Olive oil
Salt
Freshly ground pepper.

Peel the aubergines and cut them into thick slices. Sprinkle them with cooking salt and leave to sweat for 10 to 15 minutes in a sieve. Wipe them well before frying them in hot – but not boiling - oil, until they are brown. Strain them in a sieve, and put to one side.

Cook the rice in 1 l of boiling water for 11 minutes from its first boil. Drain and put to one side.

Cut the shoulder into pieces and put it through the mill with the mint, the cumin, the Cayenne pepper, 2 to 3 tablespoons of olive oil, and some salt and pepper. Place the meat in a dish and mix with the beaten eggs and the rice. Check the seasoning.

Take 6 ramekins and cover the inside with the fried slices of aubergine.

Cook the charlottes in a bain marie for about 25 minutes, and serve them hot or warm.

Chipolatas à la tomate
Tomato chipolatas

Preparation time :
20 minutes
Cooking time : 15 minutes

Ingredients for 6 :
18 chipolatas
8 to 10 ripe tomatoes
1 onion
2 garlic cloves
2 pinches of ground thyme flowers
Fresh basil
Fresh tarragon
1 bay leaf
1 pinch of caster sugar
Olive oil
Salt
Freshly ground pepper.

Grill the chipolatas (after pricking them with a fork so that they don't burst open) in a non-stick pan for 10 minutes on a slow heat. Season with salt and pepper and put to one side.

Brown the minced onions in a few tablespoons of olive oil and the garlic. Add the peeled, seeded and chopped tomatoes with 2 pinches of basil, tarragon, thyme and one of sugar. Season with salt and pepper and leave to reduce for about 15 minutes. Blend the coulis in the food processor, and pour it over the chipolatas.

Cook for another 5 minutes on a slow heat and check the seasoning.

This easy to prepare dish is served hot, sprinkled with fresh basil. Fresh pasta make a nice side dish.

Feuilleté d'escargots
Snail pastry

Preparation time :
35 minutes
Cooking time : 20 minutes

Ingredients for 6 :
500 g/1 lb or 600 g/1,3 lb of
escargots de Bourgogne (snails
from Burgundy), or failing that,
use top quality tins/cans
200 g/7 oz of cultivated mushrooms
400 g/0,8 lb of puff pastry
2 tomatoes
3 pinches of minced parsley
2 garlic cloves
2 shallots
Fresh chives
Crème fraîche or double cream
1 egg yolk
1/4 l/1/2 Pt of white wine
Butter
Salt
Freshly ground pepper

For the sauce :
The *escargots* cooking liquid
1/4 l/1/2 Pt of chicken stock
2 tablespoons of crème fraîche
or double cream
Butter
1 pinch of chives.

Mince the shallots, the mushrooms, the garlic and the parsley, and seed the tomatoes. Put to one side. Heat the *escargots* and the white wine with a pinch of thyme in a saucepan for about 7 to 8 minutes. Drain the *escargots* and keep the cooking liquid in a bowl.

Brown the shallots with one tablespoon of butter and another of olive oil. Add the mushrooms and the garlic and parsley, as well as the tomatoes, and leave to cook for 7 to 8 minutes. Throw in the *escargots* with 2 tablespoons of cream, and season with salt and pepper. Leave to simmer for 5 minutes, stir well, and put it to one side.

Meanwhile, roll out the puff pastry (it should be about 1/2 cm thick), and cut it into 6 rectangles (about 8 cm x 6 cm). Lay the *escargots* and the mushrooms equally on the centre of each *feuilletés*. Close tightly each rectangle so as to form turnovers, and brush each of them with egg yolk. Cook them in a hot oven on a buttered baking tray for 20 minutes until they are brown.

The *feuilletés* must be served as soon as they come out of the oven, and you can top them with the following sauce. Leave the *escargots* cooking liquid and 1/4 l of chicken stock to reduce by half. Add the cream, the salt and pepper, bring to the boil and away from the heat, whisk 50 g of butter in the saucepan. Add a pinch of fresh chives, and check the seasoning.

Filets de bœuf mariné
Marinated beef

Preparation time :
25 minutes and 2 h for the marinade
Cooking time : 4 minutes

Ingredients for 6 :
6 slices of beef fillets, quite thick, and about 250 g/8,5 oz each
50 g/2 oz of butter
1.5 to 2 dl/0,3 to 0,5 Pt of cognac
6 tablespoons of port wine
3 teaspoons of green pepper
1 pinch of fresh tarragon
250 g/8 oz of crème fraîche or double cream
Salt
Freshly ground pepper

For the marinade :
3/4 l/1,5 Pt of Côtes du Rhône red wine preferably
2 carrots
2 onions
2 pinches of thyme flowers
1 bay leaf.

Slice the onions and the carrots and marinate them in a hollow dish with the slices of beef, the red wine, the bay leaf, the thyme and some salt and pepper for 2 hours at least.

Drain the meat, and put it to one side, as well as about 3 dl of marinade which will later be used for the sauce.

Slowly melt 50 g of butter in a frying pan, and brown over a brisk heat the fillets, 2 minutes on each side. Season with salt and pepper, heat the cognac in a small pan, pour it over the meat and flambé.

Remove the beef from the pan and keep it warm. Meanwhile, deglaze the cooking liquid with 3 dl from the marinade and the port wine, and add the cream. Leave to reduce over a slow heat for 10 minutes.

Pour in the green pepper and check the seasoning.

Lay the meat on the plates, and top it with the sauce. You can serve the fillets with fresh pasta, buttered and sprinkled with a pinch of fresh tarragon.

Foie gras poêlé aux raisins muscats

Roasted foie gras with muscat grapes

Preparation time :
30 minutes
Cooking time : 4 minutes

Ingredients for 6 :
1 foie gras (either duck or goose), about 800 g/1,7 lb, raw
500 g/1 lb of white muscat grapes
1 dl/0,2 Pt of Madeira wine
Salt
Freshly ground pepper.

Peel and seed the grapes, and put to one side. After removing its nerves, cut the foie gras into escalopes (about 1.5 cm thick). Season with salt and pepper.

Brown the foie in a non-stick pan over a very slow heat for about 2 minutes on each side, and remove the escalopes from the pan.

Deglaze the cooking liquid with the Madeira wine. Leave to cook for about 3 to 4 minutes, and blend the sauce in the food processor. Check the seasoning. Reheat the foie gras and the grapes in the sauce.

Be very careful when cooking the escalopes, as they should still be pinkish when cooked. Prepare 2 escalopes napped with sauce and grapes for each guest.

This dish can be served as a starter or a main course.

Fricassée de foies de volaille à l'estragon

Chicken liver and tarragon fricassee

**Preparation time :
5 minutes
Cooking time : 10 minutes**

Ingredients for 6 :
800 g to 1 kg/1,7 to 2 lb
of chicken livers
1 garlic clove
A dozen of fresh tarragon
leaves
2 pinches of minced parsley
4 tablespoons of cognac
1 tablespoon of crème fraîche,
or double cream
Butter
Peanut oil
Salt
Freshly ground pepper.

Peel the garlic and crush it with a garlic press. Put it to one side. Brown the chicken livers with a tablespoon of butter and another of olive oil, for 7 to 8 minutes, stirring continuously. Season with salt and pepper and add the parsley, the garlic and the tarragon.

Then, after heating the cognac in a small pan, pour it over the livers and flambé them over a brisk heat. Turn down the heat and add the cream. Blend it well with the livers and leave to cook for 2 to 3 more minutes.

Check the seasoning.

Serve the fricassee immediately, sprinkled with a pinch of minced tarragon. You can serve sauté "fonds d'artichauts" (artichoke hearts) as a side dish.

Grives à la sauce truffée
Thrush and truffle sauce

**Preparation time :
30 minutes
Cooking time : 15 minutes**

Ingredients for 6 :
6 thrushes, plucked
6 pieces of crust
1 truffle (weighing about 30 g)
1 piece of bard
2 egg yolks
Butter
Salt
Freshly ground pepper.

Finely grate the truffle and put to one side. Don't gut the thrushes, and tie a piece of lard with a string around each of them.

Cook them in a saucepan with 50 g of butter for 10 to 15 minutes, on a medium heat, turning them over after 6 or 7 minutes. Season with salt and pepper and remove them from the casserole. Remove very carefully the inside of the birds which you will blend in the food processor, and keep the birds warm.

In the casserole, add the minced "inside" of the birds, the 2 egg yolks and the grated truffle. Beat with a fork over a very slow heat for 2 minutes, and check the seasoning.

Toast the slightly buttered pieces of crust in the oven, lay the birds on the crust, and top with the truffle preparation.

You have to be a game lover to really enjoy this dish. Try and find birds which were on grapes to make sure of the quality of the dish.

Jambon à l'os braisé à la sauge
Braised ham on the bone with sage

Preparation time :
20 minutes
Cooking time : 25 minutes

Ingredients for 6 :
6 thick slices of ham on the bone
4 shallots
2 garlic cloves
250 g/8 oz of cultivated mushrooms
1 tablespoon of wine vinegar
1 pinch of ground thyme
2 pinches of minced parsley
3 pinches of dried sage preferably (as it looses its bitterness when drying)
1/2 l/1 Pt of dry white wine
Butter
2 tablespoons of crème fraîche or double cream
Salt
Freshly ground pepper.

Peel and mince the shallots, the garlic and the mushrooms. Mince the parsley and put to one side. Cook the shallots in a saucepan with the vinegar, over a slow heat until the vinegar is totally evaporated. Add a tablespoon of butter, the mushrooms, the parsley, the garlic, the thyme and the sage, as well as the white wine.

Cook over a slow heat until the wine is totally reduced. Add the cream, and season with salt and pepper. Keep the sauce warm. You can blend it very quickly in the food processor so that there still are a few pieces.

Butter an oven dish and lay the slices of ham inside. Pour the rest of the wine over them and cover carefully the dish with foil. Cook in a hot oven for about 20 to 25 minutes.

Take the braised ham out from the oven. Pour the cooking liquid in the sage sauce, heat up, and away from the heat, whisk in 50 g of butter. Pour the sauce over the ham. Serve immediately.

You can serve the ham with steamed potatoes or green lentil purée.

Lapin aux olives
Rabbit and olives

Preparation time:
10 minutes
Cooking time : 55 minutes

Ingredients for 6 :
A rabbit, weighing about 1.5
to 2 kg/3 to 4 lb,
2 onions
150 g/5 oz of smoked bacon
150 g/5 oz of green and black
olives, stoned
3 garlic cloves
2 pinches of ground thyme
flowers
3 pinches of fresh parsley
1 dl/0,2 Pt of dry white wine
1 small glass of cognac
1 dl/0,2 Pt of water
1 tablespoon of cornflour
Olive oil
Salt
Freshly ground pepper.

Brown the sliced onion and the smoked bacon with a few tablespoons of olive oil, over a slow heat. Add the pieces of rabbit, which should be browned on each side, and cook for 10 to 15 minutes.

Flambé with the cognac, and season with salt and pepper.

Add the white wine, the water, the olives, the garlic cloves and the thyme. Leave to simmer, uncovered, for 40 minutes.

Thicken the sauce by mixing it with 1 tablespoon of cornflour diluted in 1 tablespoon of water. Whisk over a very slow heat, and check the seasoning.

You can serve the pieces of rabbit napped with the sauce and sprinkled with fresh parsley, and with fresh pasta as a side dish.

Paupiettes de veau à la niçoise
Veal olives a la Nicoise

Preparation time :
30 minutes
Cooking time : 45 minutes

Ingredients for 6 :
12 veal escalopes (weighing
about 50 g/1,7 oz each)
150 g/5 oz of cooked ham
150 g/5 oz of stoned
black olives
3 garlic cloves
7 or 8 twigs of parsley
Thyme
1.5 dl/0,2 Pt of dry white wine
3 ripe tomatoes
The juice of half a lemon
3 tablespoons of crème
fraîche or double cream
Olive oil
Salt
Freshly ground pepper.

Flatten the escalopes, and season them with salt and pepper. Put the ham, the garlic, the parsley and half the black olives through the mill. It will constitute the stuffing.

Share the stuffing into 6 parts, and place on the escalopes. Season with pepper, but not with salt, as the ham and the olives can be very salty. Roll the veal olives and tie each of them to its extremities with string.

Heat a few tablespoons of olive oil in a casserole, and brown the veal olives for 5 to 6 minutes over a brisk heat. Add the tomatoes, the rest of the olives, a pinch of ground thyme, the white wine, a tablespoon of water and the lemon juice.

Leave to simmer for about 30 minutes and pour in the cream. Stir well so that the cream is mixed with the other ingredients, and leave to cook for another 10 minutes. Check the seasoning and serve hot.

The veal olives can be cooked one day beforehand, as they only taste better when reheated. Serve a fresh garden pea purée as a side dish.

Perdreaux aux échalottes
Partridge and shallots

Preparation time :
20 minutes
Cooking time : 45 minutes

Ingredients for 6 :
3 partridges
12 shallots
12 garlic cloves
2 pinches of fresh thyme
A piece of bard
Butter
Peanut oil
1 dl/0,2 Pt of chicken stock
Salt
Freshly ground pepper.

Season with salt and pepper the inside of the partridge and cover with a piece of bard. Brown them with a mixing of butter and oil and 2 pinches of thyme in a casserole dish, for 7 to 8 minutes on each side.

Season with salt and pepper. Add the whole peeled shallots and the washed but not peeled garlic cloves.

Pour in the chicken stock and the wine. Cover and leave to simmer for about 1/2 hour until the shallots are smooth. Check the seasoning.

Serve half a partridge for each guest, topped with juice, and smooth shallots and garlic around the game. You can serve it with roasted strips of green cabbage or a lentil purée.

Poulet farci à l'ail nouveau et au thym

Chicken stuffed with new garlic and thyme

Preparation time :
10 minutes
Cooking time : 45 minutes

Ingredients for 6 :
1 chicken (weighing 1.5 to 2 kg/3 to 4 lb)
4 to 5 pinches of ground thyme flowers
8 cloves of new garlic
1 dl/0,2 Pt of olive oil
Butter
3 pieces of crust, rubbed with garlic
Salt
Freshly ground pepper.

Mix 3 or 4 pinches of ground thyme with the crushed garlic, and 50 g of soft butter. Season the inside of the chicken with salt and pepper and stuff it with this preparation as well as with the crust rubbed with garlic.

In a glass, blend the rest of thyme with the olive oil, and brush the chicken with this mixture. Season once again and cook it in a hot oven for 45 minutes, basting it from time to time with the olive oil.

The chicken prepared in this way has a savoury flesh, delicately flavoured with garlic. You can serve a green salad and the *croûtons* (the pieces of bread cooked inside the chicken) as a side dish.

Rognons et ris de veau aux cèpes
Kidney and calf sweetbread with ceps

Preparation time :
35 minutes (but the calf sweetbread must be soaked one day beforehand)
Cooking time : 7 minutes

Ingredients for 6 :
About 600 g/1,3 lb of calf 's kidney
500 g/1 lb of calf sweetbread
800 g/1,7 lb of ceps
4 shallots
1 pinch of fresh chives
1 pinch of parsley
Butter
Oil
Salt
Freshly ground pepper.

When the sweetbread has soaked in cold water with a pinch of salt for one night in the fridge, throw it in a saucepan filled with cold water, and bring it to the boil for 5 minutes. Put it back in cold water for another 10 minutes. Wipe it and slice it into 1 cm thick slices, and put to one side.

Slice the shallots and the ceps. Mince the parsley and the chives and slice the kidney. Put to one side.

Brown the shallots in 25 g of butter over a slow heat until they are soft and translucent. Add 2 tablespoons of olive oil and 20 g of butter, throw in the ceps, season with salt, pepper and sauté them for about 10 minutes over a medium heat. Sprinkle with chives and put to one side.

Brown the salted and peppered slices of kidney and sweetbread in two different frying pans with a blending oil and butter for about 2 minutes.

Serve immediately the kidney and the sweetbread, topped with the sweetbread cooking butter and the ceps. This recipe is very easy to follow. The quality of the product is a guaranty for its success. For lack of ceps, you can serve this dish with chanterelles or any other variety of mushrooms.

Saucisson de viande
Large meat sausage

**Preparation time :
35 minutes
Cooking time : 40 minutes**

Ingredients for 6 :
350 g/11 oz of veal eye
350 g/11 oz of pork chine,
boned
150 g/5 oz of fresh belly of
pork
1 piece of caul of pork
1 onion
2 cloves of garlic
200 g/6 oz of cultivated
mushrooms
2 eggs
2 tablespoons of crème
fraîche or double cream
Chives
6 to 7 twigs of parsley
2 to 3 dried sage leaves
Salt
Freshly ground pepper
5 to 6 green peppercorns.

Soak the caul in a pan filled with cold water for 15 minutes, and put to one side. Mince the chine, smoked belly of pork, and veal, with the parsley, the garlic, the onion, the chives, and the sage, and put to one side.

Brown the sliced mushrooms with 2 tablespoons of olive oil and 25 g of butter over a slow heat. Add a little salt, the pepper and the minced parsley, and put to one side.

In a large mixing bowl, mix the minced meat, the mushrooms, the beaten eggs, and a little salt and pepper. Knead this mixture, and give it the shape of a *saucisson* (a large sausage)

Drain the caul, lay it down onto the working surface and fill it with the stuffing. Tie the extremities and place this *saucisson* in a slightly buttered dish. Cook it in a hot oven for about 40 minutes.

Remove the excess fat expressed from the caul, and deglaze the cooking liquid with 1/2 glass of water, the cream, a little salt and some green pepper. Put this sauce through the food processor. Serve the sliced *saucisson* topped with the sauce described previously. If possible, slice the sausage with an electric knife.

Terrine de foies de volailles aux olives noires

Chicken liver and black olives pâté

Preparation time :
20 minutes
Cooking time : 6 minutes

Ingredients for 6 :
250 g/8 oz of black olives, stoned
250 g/8 oz of chicken liver
150 g/5 oz of soft butter
3 tablespoons of port wine
1 pinch of allspice
1 pinch of ground nutmeg
Butter
Peanut oil
Salt
Freshly ground pepper.

Finely mince the black olives. Put to one side. Brown the sliced onions with a tablespoon of butter, and 2 tablespoons of oil for 4 to 5 minutes. Add the chicken livers, and cook for another 5 to 6 minutes, moving them around in the pan.

Mix the livers in the food processor with the onions, the port wine, the ground nutmeg, the pepper and very little salt.

Add, manually this time, the softened butter blended with the minced olives, until the paste is smooth. Check the seasoning.

Fill a tureen with the preparation and place in the fridge for the next 3 hours at least.

This dish is very tasty, but you have however to be careful with the livers, as they should stay underdone, as they would lose all their flavour if cooked for too long. You can serve it as a starter with toasts and "oignons glacés" (you can find this recipe in the *Vegetables* chapter), or more simply, with a green salad.

Tourte de canard à l'estragon
Duck and tarragon pie

Preparation time :
2 hours
Cooking time : 25 minutes

Ingredients for 6 :
1 duck (about 2 kg/4 lb)
1 big onion
100 g/3,5 oz of green olives
250 g/8 oz of fresh cultivated mushrooms or any other variety
A little aniseed
A dozen of fresh tarragon leaves
1 pinch of freshly minced chives
Salt
Freshly ground pepper
Butter
Peanut or sunflower oil
400 g/15 oz of puff pastry
1 egg yolk.

Roast the duck for an hour and a half in a slow oven, taking care to baste it frequently with the mixture of butter and oil when it cooks. Deglaze the cooking liquid with 1/2 glass of hot water, and put to one side.

When the duck has cooled down, remove the flesh from the bones. Cut up the cutlets, the flesh from the feet and the drumsticks, in the shape of "aiguillettes", and put to one side.

Brown the sliced onion and mushrooms with one tablespoon of butter and 3 of oil for about 10 minutes. Season with salt and pepper, the tarragon, which is the main herb in this recipe, the aniseed, the minced chives, the green olives, as well as a few tablespoons of the cooking liquid. Mix and check the seasoning, put to one side.

Roll the puff pastry and lay it down in a pie plate. Prick it with a fork and fill with the meat. Cover with a layer of pastry, brush with a little egg yolk and cook the pie for about 25 minutes in a hot oven until it is brown.

This pie is served hot. You might top it with a "crème de champignon", the recipe of which you can find in the *sauces* chapter.

Veau aux asperges
Veal and asparagus

Preparation time :
35 minutes
Cooking time : 1 h 50

Ingredients for 6 :
1.5 kg/3 lb of veal eye
1 bunch of spring onions
1 bunch of asparagus tips
(about 500 g/1 lb)
1 bouquet garni
1/2 l/1 Pt of meat stock
2 tablespoons of cream
1.5 dl/0,2 Pt of dry white wine
2 pinches of minced parsley
Oil
Butter
Salt
Freshly ground pepper.

In a saucepan, brown the veal eye with 50 g of butter and 2 tablespoons of peanut oil, a little salt and pepper and the spring onions for 15 to 20 minutes over a medium heat. Add 1/2 l of stock, a glass of white wine, and the bouquet garni. Cover, and leave to simmer for 1h30.

Meanwhile, cooked the peeled asparagus in salted boiling water for 25 minutes. Drain and add to the meat, as well as 2 tablespoons of cream, and leave to simmer for another 5 minutes. Check the seasoning.

Slice the meat, top it with the sauce, and sprinkle with minced parsley.

Veau aux cèpes
Veal with ceps

Preparation time :
25 minutes
Cooking time : 45 minutes

Ingredients for 6 :
1.5 kg/3 lb of veal fillet
300 g/10 oz of fresh ceps, or
failing that, 2 handfuls of dry
ones
4 shallots
4 pinches of minced parsley
150 g/5 oz of cream
1.5 dl/0,2 Pt of dry white wine
Olive oil
Butter
Salt
Freshly ground pepper.

Sweat the sliced shallots with a tablespoon of olive oil in a casserole dish. Add the veal, which you should brown on its sides, and cook over a medium heat for 25 to 30 minutes until it is brown. Season with salt and pepper.

Meanwhile, brown the sliced ceps in 2 tablespoons of butter and one of oil for 10 minutes. Season with salt and pepper, add 2 pinches of minced parsley, and put to one side.

Remove the meat from the pan and keep it warm.

Deglaze the cooking liquid with the white wine and stir well, so as to mix all the juices. Throw the ceps in the casserole dish with the cream. Put back the meat, and leave to simmer for another 15 minutes.

Cut the fillet in thick slices, and top it with the sauce and the ceps, sprinkled with minced parsley.

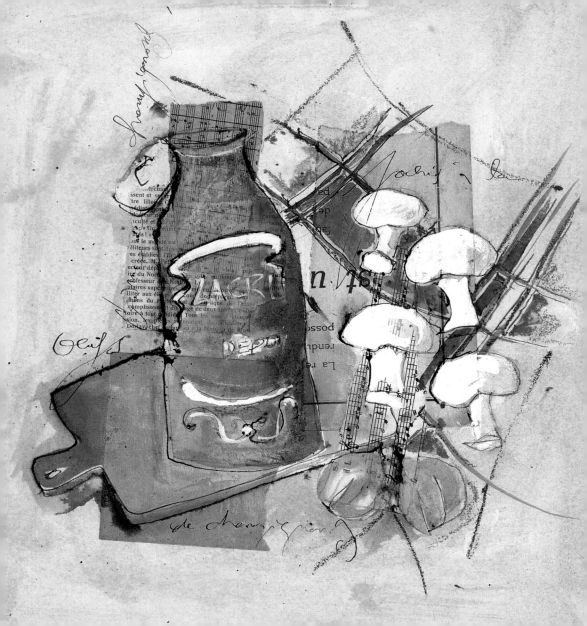

Sauces

Aïoli

Preparation time :
15 minutes

Ingredients for 6 :
5 garlic cloves
2 egg yolks
1/2 teaspoon of English
mustard
About 3 dl/0,4 Pt of olive oil
The juice of 1/2 lemon
Salt
Freshly ground pepper.

Peel the garlic cloves and remove the eyes, and crush them using a mortar or a garlic press. Throw the garlic purée in a mixing bowl, add the mustard, a pinch of salt, a pinch of pepper, and the egg yolks (it is preferable for all the ingredients to be at the same temperature).

Pour a dash of olive oil and begin to whisk with an electric whisk preferably, until the preparation thickens.

Pour the olive oil continuously, until you have enough for your recipe (you can pour in 1/2 l of oil for the mentioned quantity of ingredients). The consistency of this sauce should be thick, like a mayonnaise.

Add the juice of 1/2 lemon, give it a good stir, check the seasoning and store the sauce in the fridge.

This sauce is very popular in Provence, and is traditionally served with "bouillabaisse", but you can serve it with a number of meats, cold fish, pâtés, salads, etc.

Anchoïade

Preparation time :
25 minutes
Cooking time : 25 minutes

Ingredients for 6 :
12 salted fillets of anchovies
8 garlic cloves
A dash of wine vinegar
About 1/4 l/1/2 Pt of olive oil
Freshly ground pepper.

Cook the garlic cloves in their cloves in a hot oven for about 20 to 30 minutes in a slightly buttered dish. Leave them to cool down, peel them and mash them with a fork so as to get a purée. Put to one side.

Meanwhile, clean the anchovies, remove the central bone and soak them in cold water. Cook them in a casserole with 3 to 4 tablespoons of olive oil, and 2 pinches of freshly ground pepper over a very slow heat.

Stir gently until it forms a *pommade*. Add the garlic purée, give it a good stir and add the rest of the oil and the dash of vinegar away from the heat.

This sauce is served hot or cold, with raw vegetables such as celery, chicory, curly endive, cardoons, cauliflower or carrots.

This sauce is called *pébrade* in Provence and can be stored in a jar, in the fidge for a few weeks. You can use it as a dressing for curly endive. It can also season a cold potato salad.

Beurre provençal
Provencal butter

Preparation : 10 minutes

Ingredients for 6 :
100 g/3,5 oz of butter
2 garlic cloves
2 shallots
6 capers
1 pinch of freshly minced parsley
1 pinch of freshly minced tarragon
1 pinch of freshly minced chervil
Salt
Freshly ground pepper.

Peel the garlic cloves and crush them with garlic press. Slice the shallots. Mix the garlic, the herbs, the shallots, the capers, and a little salt and pepper with the soft butter.

Knead the preparation and give it the form of a roller, and store in the fridge. Slice it finely just before you serve it.

The *beurre provençal* can be used cold to top potatoes cooked in embers or warm on brochettes of meat or fish.

Coulis de tomates
Tomato purée

**Preparation time :
15 minutes
Cooking time : 15 minutes**

Ingredients for 6 :
1 kg/2 lb of ripe tomatoes
1 onion
2 garlic cloves
Fresh basil
Fresh tarragon
Oregano
Thyme
Fresh chives
1 bay leaf
1 pinch of sugar
Olive oil
Freshly ground pepper.

Peel and seed the tomatoes, chop them and put them to one side.

Brown the minced onion and garlic in 4 tablespoons of oil for 3 to 4 minutes over a slow heat. Add the tomatoes and a pinch of minced basil, tarragon and chives, a little less oregano and thyme, a pinch of sugar, and a little salt and pepper.

Leave the preparation to reduce for about 10 minutes. Mix the tomatoes in the food processor. You should then have a smooth coulis, with an almost orange colour, which you can serve hot or cold.

The *coulis de tomates* is a base for the Provencal cuisine. It can top a fish, a vegetable *gâteau*, a pâté or pasta.

Try and always store some in the freezer, in an ice tray as it is very practical, and easy to defrost. You can then take some out as you need it.

Crème d'ail

Preparation time :
15 minutes
Cooking time : 30 minutes

Ingredients for 6 :
5 heads of white garlic (as it is less strong)
25 cl/0,5 Pt of chicken stock
150 g/5 oz of cream
6 basil leaves
1 pinch of thyme flowers
Butter
Olive oil
Freshly ground pepper.

Blanch the peeled garlic cloves in half a litre of water for about 5 minutes (you can change the water twice during the cooking). Drain the cloves.

Place the garlic in a large square of foil, sprinkle it with 2 tablespoon of olive oil, and a pinch of sugar. Close tightly and cook in a hot oven for 15 minutes.

Throw the cooked garlic in a saucepan with the chicken stock, the cream, the basil, the salt, the pepper and the thyme. Crush it all and give it a good stir. Cook for 15 minutes, and add, away from the fire, 30 g of butter. Mix it in the food processor, and check the seasoning.

This sauce is served hot with grilled meats or roasted beef, pork and, above all, lamb.

Crème de champignons
Mushroom cream

Preparation time :
15 minutes
Cooking time : 15 minutes

Ingredients for 6 :
300 g/10 oz of fresh cultivated mushrooms
1 shallot
1 tablespoon of crème fraîche
or double cream
1 teaspoon of cornflour
2 dl/0,5 Pt of chicken stock
Butter
Salt
Freshly ground pepper.

Peel the shallot and the mushrooms and finely mince them. Sweat them with 3 tablespoons of butter for 10 minutes. Season with salt and pepper and put to one side.

Melt 1 tablespoon of butter in a saucepan, add 1 teaspoon of cornflour, stirring quickly so as to blend the two ingredients. Add little by little the warm chicken stock, and, stirring continuously, simmer for 3 to 4 minutes until the sauce thickens. Add a little salt, not too much because of the stock, and some pepper.

Mix the shallot and the mushrooms in the sauce. Add a tablespoon of cream and bring to the boil. Check the seasoning.

This mushroom sauce is served hot, with poultry and roasted white or red meats.

Crème de poivrons rouges
Cream of red peppers

Preparation time :
15 minutes
Cooking time : 30 minutes

Ingredients for 6 :
500 to 600 g/1 lb to 1,3 lb
of red peppers
1 big onion
2 garlic cloves
4 ripe tomatoes, peeled and
seeded
50 g/2 oz of crème fraîche or
double cream
Olive oil
1 pinch of sugar
1.5 dl/0,2 Pt of water
Salt
Freshly ground pepper.

Brown the minced onion and garlic with 3 tablespoons of olive oil over a slow heat until they change colour.

Meanwhile, seed the peppers and dice them. Throw them in a saucepan with the onions, add the tomatoes, season with salt and pepper and add the water. Bring to the boil, then cover and cook for half an hour.

Pour the preparation in a food processor with the cream and the pinch of sugar. Blend and check the seasoning.

Serve warm. This smooth cream can be served with grilled fish, or the egg based preparations, such as an omelette or a "gâteau d'asperges" (see the recipe in the *Vegetables* chapter).

Rouille

**Preparation time :
10 minutes**

Ingredients for 6 :
4 garlic cloves
3 chilli peppers or the quarter
of a teaspoon of red hot peppers purée
1/2 a handful of the white
part of a bread
3 tablespoons of milk
3 tablespoons of olive oil
0.5 dl/0,1 Pt of fish stock
1 teaspoon of tomato purée
Salt
Freshly ground pepper
A piece of a gilt-head liver
(optional).

Peel the garlic cloves and crush them with a garlic press. Soak about half a handful of the white part of a bread in the milk, and crush with a fork.

Mix the garlic pulp with the crushed peppers and the soaked bread, and add 2 to 3 tablespoons of olive oil, the tomato purée, a little salt and pepper and finally the fish stock. Whisk the preparation until the sauce is smooth.

You can pound and add to the preparation the liver of a fish (a gilt-head preferably), and a teaspoon of tomato purée.

This sauce can be served with bouillabaisse and any fish soup. It is served cold and should be a little hot (you can put more or less pepper if you want).

Sauce à l'estragon

Tarragon sauce

Preparation time :
5 minutes
Cooking time :
about 15 minutes

Ingredients for 6 :
4 minced shallots
3 tablespoons of wine vinegar
12 minced leaves of tarragon
1/4 l/1/2 Pt of dry white wine
2 tablespoons of crème fraîche or double cream
100 g/3,5 oz of butter
Salt
Freshly ground pepper.

Peel and mince finely the shallots. Throw them in a saucepan with the vinegar. Leave this preparation to reduce until the vinegar is totally evaporated.

Add the wine, leave to reduce one more time, and pour in the cream. Bring to the boil and incorporate the butter, little by little and away from the heat, with a whisk. Finally, add the tarragon and a little salt and pepper.

This sauce can be served with roasted fish as well as fried or roasted meats.

Sauce aux fines herbes
Fines herbes sauce

Preparation time :
10 minutes

Ingredients for 6 :
125 g/4 oz of crème fraîche or
double cream
1 teaspoon of mustard
2 twigs of chervil
7 to 8 fresh leaves of basil
7 to 8 fresh leaves of tarragon
5 to 6 twigs of fresh chives
A little Cayenne pepper
1 tablespoon of lemon juice
Salt
Freshly ground pepper.

Finely mince the fines herbes. In a mixing bowl, mix the mustard with the cream, the fines herbes, the lemon juice, the Cayenne pepper, and the salt and pepper.

This sauce is served cold with cold fish pâtés or with crudités such as cucumber, asparagus, etc.

Sauce aux tomates crues

Raw tomato sauce

Preparation time :
10 minutes

Ingredients for 6 :
6 big and ripe tomatoes
3 tablespoons of crème
fraîche or double cream
1 pinch of freshly minced basil
1 pinch of freshly minced
chervil
1 mince of freshly minced tarragon
1 pinch of minced parsley
Salt
Freshly ground pepper.

Peel the tomatoes, mix them in the food processor with the cream, the parsley, the basil, the tarragon, and the salt and pepper. Check the seasoning.

This raw tomato "coulis" is served chilled with, as a fruity sauce, grilled fish, You can top a warm tomato "flan" with this sauce (you can find this recipe in the *Vegetables* chapter.)

Sauce chaude aux anchois

Hot anchovy sauce

Preparation time :
10 minutes
Cooking time : 7 minutes

Ingredients for 6 :
15 soaked fillets of anchovies
2 garlic cloves
2 tablespoons of cream
2 tablespoons of wine vinegar
Olive oil
150 g/5 oz of butter
Salt
Freshly ground pepper.

Slowly cook the anchovies with 3 tablespoons of olive oil mixed with the crushed garlic. Mix well until it has the consistency of a purée, then add the vinegar and leave to cook for 3 or 4 minutes

Pour in the cream, bring to the boil and whisk in, away from the fire, the pieces of butter. Pepper, and check the seasoning.

This sauce can be served with a roasted beef fillet.

Sauce safranée
Saffron sauce

Preparation time :
5 minutes
Cooking time : 10 minutes

Ingredients for 6 :
1 shallot
2 tablespoons of cream
3 dl/0,4 Pt of fish stock
50 g/2,5 oz of butter
1 pinch of saffron
Salt, freshly ground pepper.

Peel the shallot and slice it finely. Brown it with a knob of butter over a slow heat. Add the stock, leave to reduce for 5 to 6 minutes and add the cream. Season with salt and pepper and cook for another 3 to 4 minutes.

Whisk in the butter, away from the heat, and add a pinch of saffron. Check the seasoning and serve hot.

This sauce can be served with a *feuilleté de poisson* or a *poisson en papillotte*.

Sauce vinaigrette

———•○○)⟩)⟩○○•———

**Preparation time :
3 minutes**

Ingredients for 6 :
1 clove of purple garlic,
2 cloves of white garlic,
(the eye of which you should remove)
A dash of wine vinegar
2 pinches of minced chives
Olive oil
Salt
Freshly ground pepper.

Peel the garlic cloves, remove the eye, and crush them in a garlic press. Throw the garlic purée in a mixing bowl, add the dash of vinegar, the chives, the pepper, stir well, then whisk the preparation for a minute.

Throw the drained salad in a bowl, and only then, add the salt. Mix well, and serve immediately.

This garlic vinaigrette can be served with green salads, and especially curly endives. You can also serve it on a tomato salad.

Tapenade

Preparation time :
15 minutes

Ingredients for 6 :
200 g/7 oz of black olives,
(from Nyons if possible),
stoned if possible
8 salted fillets of anchovies
10 fresh leaves of basil
3 pinches of capers preserved
in vinegar
About 5 cl/0,1 Pt of olive oil
Freshly ground pepper.

Clean the fillets, remove the central bone, and soak them in cold water. Mix them in a food processor with the stoned olives, the capers, the pepper, the basil, the garlic and as much olive oil as you judge necessary, bearing in mind that it should be thick, and check the seasoning.

The tapenade is an olive purée which can be served with a great number of variegated dishes.

I've had the opportunity to enjoy, as an appetizer, a superposition of 3 layers of mayonnaise, coulis de tomates and tapenade, served in a small glass, so that the layers are visible. Try and taste it, as it is nice and delicious.

You can garnish small rectangles of puff pastry with the tapenade. The feuilletés should then be served as a starter with a green salad.

You can also stuff saltwater fish with one or two tablespoons of tapenade before you braise them in an oven, or you can mix them with fresh pasta.

Finally, you can preserve some tapenade in a jar and store it in a fridge for a few weeks.

Desserts
Puddings

Beignets d'abricots
Apricot fritters

Preparation time :
25 minutes + 30 minutes
for the batter to stand
Cooking time : 15 times

Ingredients for 6 :
1 dozen of apricots
225 g/8 oz of flour
2 egg yolks
2 egg whites
2 tablespoons of oil
2 dl/0,5 Pt of water
1 pinch of salt
1 pinch of vanilla
Caster sugar
3 tablespoons of kirsch
1 l/2 Pt of frying oil.

In a mixing bowl, mix the flour, the salt, the egg yolks and the oil. Slowly pour in the warm water until the batter is smooth and thin. Leave it to stand for half an hour.

Meanwhile, open the apricots, and remove the stones. Throw them in a mixing bowl and sprinkle them with 5 to 6 tablespoons of sugar, the vanilla, and the kirsch. Mix well, and leave to macerate for 15 minutes.

Add the firmly whisked egg whites to the batter. Then, dip each the apricot halves into the batter and deep fry them in the hot but not boiling frying oil until the fritters brown.

Drain and sprinkle with caster sugar.

Cerises aux épices
Cherries and spice

Preparation time :
30 minutes
Cooking time : 20 minutes

Ingredients for 6 :
1 kg/2 lb of black cherries
1/4 l/1/2 Pt of water
100 g/3,5 oz of sugar
2 pinches of vanilla
1 pinch of cinnamon
1 pinch of ground nutmeg
1 clove
The peel of an orange
4 to 5 fresh leaves of mint
1 glass of Malaga wine.

Bring to the boil the water and the sugar and all the spices. Leave to simmer for 10 minutes, cover, and leave to infuse for 10 minutes.

Meanwhile, stone the cherries, throw them in the syrup, bring to the boil, and leave to cook for 15 to 20 minutes over a slow heat. Remove from the heat and pour the Malaga wine in the saucepan. Leave to cool down and store the preparation in the store.

This dish should be served chilled, and you can serve them with a vanilla cream.

Chichis

Preparation time :
10 minutes + 1 hour for the
batter to stand
Cooking time :
4 to 5 minutes

Ingredients for 6 :
500 g/1 lb of flour
1/2 sachet of baking powder
2 tablespoons of orange
blossom water
1 dl/0,2 Pt of warm water
1 pinch of salt
2 sachets of vanilla sugar
1 1/2 Pt of frying oil.

In a mixing bowl, dilute the baking powder with a few tablespoons of water, and mix it with the flour, the salt, the orange blossom water, the vanilla sugar and the warm water.

The batter consistency should be thin and smooth. Leave it to stand for an hour in a warm place.

Cut the batter into long strips (about 20 cm x 7 cm), and deep fry them in hot but not boiling oil for 3 to 4 minutes until they change colour.

Absorb the excess oil with kitchen paper, and roll them immediately in the caster sugar.

Like all fritters, the *chichis* need to be served as soon as they are cooked. You can still find them in Provence for the village fêtes in Provence.

Clafoutis aux abricots
Apricot clafoutis

Preparation time :
25 minutes + 30 minutes
for the batter to stand
Cooking time : 40 minutes

Ingredients for 6 :
800 g/1,7 lb of ripe apricots
100 g/3,5 oz of thin honey

For the batter :
300 g/10 oz of flour
125 g/4 oz of butter
100 g/3,5 oz of sugar
5 egg yolks

For the filling :
2 egg yolks
2 whole eggs
100 g/3,5 oz of caster sugar
1 tablespoon of flour
250 g/8 oz of crème fraîche.

Open the apricots and remove the stones. Heat up the honey in a non-stick pan and throw in the halves when the honey changes colour. Brown them over a slow heat for 10 minutes until they are slightly coloured. Drain.

In a mixing bowl, knead the soft butter with the sugar. Add the egg yolks and the flour slowly, and knead again. As the paste is sticky, roll it in a little flour and leave it to stand for half an hour in the fridge.

Take the paste out of the fridge, roll it out on the floured working surface and lay it down in a pie plate.

Whisk the 2 eggs and the 2 egg yolks with the sugar, the flour and the cream.

Lay down the apricots in the pie plate and pour in the filling. Cook in a hot oven for about 30 minutes.

This clafoutis should be served warm, sprinkled with icing sugar.

Coulis de fraises
Strawberry coulis

Preparation time :
10 minutes

Ingredients for 6 :
400 g/15 oz of strawberries
4 tablespoons of caster sugar
4 tablespoons of crème
fraîche or double cream.

Remove the stalks and wash them quickly in a sieve without soaking them in the water.

Mix the strawberries for 2 minutes in a food processor with the cream, so that the coulis is smooth.

This coulis can be served by itself as a dessert. You can also pour it over fromage frais or a vanilla or strawberry ice-cream. It's a very quick dessert and it enhances the flavour of any ice-cream.

Crème caramel à la cannelle
Cinnamon and caramel cream

Preparation time :
15 minutes
Cooking time : 40 minutes

Ingredients for 6 :
3/4 l/1,5 Pt of whole milk
7 eggs
3 egg yolks
1/4 l/1/2 Pt of liquid cream
10 tablespoons of caster sugar
A piece of the peel of a lime
A pinch of cinnamon
10 lumps of sugar
The juice of half a lemon.

Heat up the cream and milk in a saucepan and add a pinch of vanilla, a pinch of cinnamon, and the lemon peel. Bring to the boil, remove from the heat and put to one side.

Heat up the lumps of sugar with 2 to 3 tablespoons of water in a small saucepan and add the lemon juice. Heat up until the caramels bowns.

Meanwhile, whisk the eggs and the sugar in the food processor and pour in the boiling milk, taking care to remove the peel of orange. Give it a stir. As soon as the caramel is ready, pour it in an oven dish, with the fillings on top.

Cook the crème in a bain marie for 35 to 40 minutes in a hot oven. Remove the dish from the oven and leave it to cool down before you turn it over.

This dessert should be served chilled, and you can prepare it one day beforehand.

Flan des vendangeurs
Vintage flan

**Preparation time :
30 minutes
Cooking time : 30 minutes**

Ingredients for 6 :
3/4 l/1,5 Pt of whole milk
1 pinch of vanilla
6 whole eggs
2 egg yolks
9 tablespoons of caster sugar
30 g/1 oz of butter
2 to 3 bunches of grapes
("chasselas" variety, if possible).

Peel and seed the grapes and lay a small handful in 6 buttered oven ramekins. Whisk the eggs and the sugar in the food processor, then add the boiling milk with vanilla, mix well, and pour in the ramekins.

Cook in a bain marie in a hot oven for about 30 minutes.

Take the flans out of the oven, leave them to cool down and store them in the fridge. They should be served chilled.

Fraises au vin rouge
Strawberries and red wine

Preparation time :
20 minutes
Cooking time : 2 h for the marinade

Ingredients for 6 :
1 kg/2 lb of strawberries
1/2 bottle of nice red wine
3 to 4 tablespoons of water
2 tablespoons of caster sugar
2 oranges
4 tablespoons of "cointreau"
1 portion of ice cream for each guest.

Wash the fruits and remove the stalks. Throw 250 g of strawberries in a bowl, add the wine, the water, the sugar and the "cointreau", mix and add the finely sliced oranges. Store the rest of the fruits, sprinkled with sugar, in the fridge.

Mix the sugared strawberries and the macerated ones, and serve.

Top each portion of ice cream with 2 tablespoons of the *marinade* and the strawberries.

This dessert should be served chilled.

Fruits chauds d'hiver en papillote
Warm winter fruits in papillote

Preparation time :
15 minutes
Cooking time : 8 minutes

Ingredients for 6 :
6 bananas
3 apples
50 g/2 oz of raisins
Caster sugar
Cinnamon
50 g/2 oz of butter
2 to 3 tablespoons of rum.

Peel the apples, slice them finely, sprinkle with 2 tablespoons of sugar and brown in a frying pan with 2 tablespoons of butter, the raisins, and the rum for 7 to 8 minutes.

Butter 6 rectangles of foil on which you will place a banana, cut into two, lengthwise. Sprinkle it with sugar and a dash of rum, a few slices of cooked apples and raisins, a pinch of cinnamon, and a knob of butter.

Close the *papillote* tightly and cook in a hot oven for 8 minutes.

Remove from the oven and serve immediately. This dessert is easy and quick to prepare. According to the season, you can prepare it with any other fruit.

Gâteau au chocolat de grand-mère Yvonne

Grand-mère Yvonne's chocolate cake

**Preparation time :
15 minutes
Cooking time : 25 minutes**

Ingredients for 6 :
200 g/7 oz of cooking chocolate
1 tablespoon of flour
1/2 sachet of baking powder
120 g/4 oz of caster sugar
100 g/3,5 oz of butter
3 eggs.

Melt the chocolate with 2 tablespoons of water in a saucepan over a slow heat, stirring constantly until it is smooth. Then, add the pieces of butter, and give it a good stir. Remove the saucepan from the heat.

Whisk the egg yolks with the sugar and mix well with the melted chocolate. Add the baking powder, the flour, mix with a wooden spoon, and incorporate the firmly whisked whites in the preparation.

Butter a tin and pour in the preparation. Cook for 20 to 25 minutes in the oven. This cake shouldn't be over cooked, as it wants to be smooth. Check whether it is cooked or not with the point of a knife : It should come out clean on the edges, whereas a little chocolate should stick on it on the centre.

This cake is easy to make and is served chilled. You could also top it with custard or a sauce of raw orange.

Gratin de framboises au sabayon
Raspberry gratin with zabaglione

Preparation time :
20 minutes
Cooking time : 3 to 4
minutes

Ingredients for 6 :
750 g/1,5 lb of raspberries

For the zabaglione :
6 egg yolks
80 g/3 oz of sugar
1 pinch of flour
4 tablespoons of water
4 tablespoons of dry white
wine
4 tablespoons of orange juice
1/2 l/1 Pt of single cream
2 tablespoons of raspberry
brandy.

Whisk the egg yolks, the flour, the sugar, the water, the wine and the orange juice in a bowl au bain marie, over a slow heat until the mixture becomes creamy and smooth (use an electric whisk if you want it to be quicker). Leave to cool down, incorporate the raspberry brandy and put to one side.

Lay the raspberries in a buttered gratin dish. Whisk the cream Chantilly and add it to the cold zabaglione.

Pour the preparation over the fruits and brown under the grill for 3 to 4 minutes. Serve immediately.

You can prepare this gratin with a variety of mixed vegetables (kiwis, mangos, bananas, strawberries, cherries, etc.) or only with red fruits (strawberries, raspberries, cherries, red currants…).

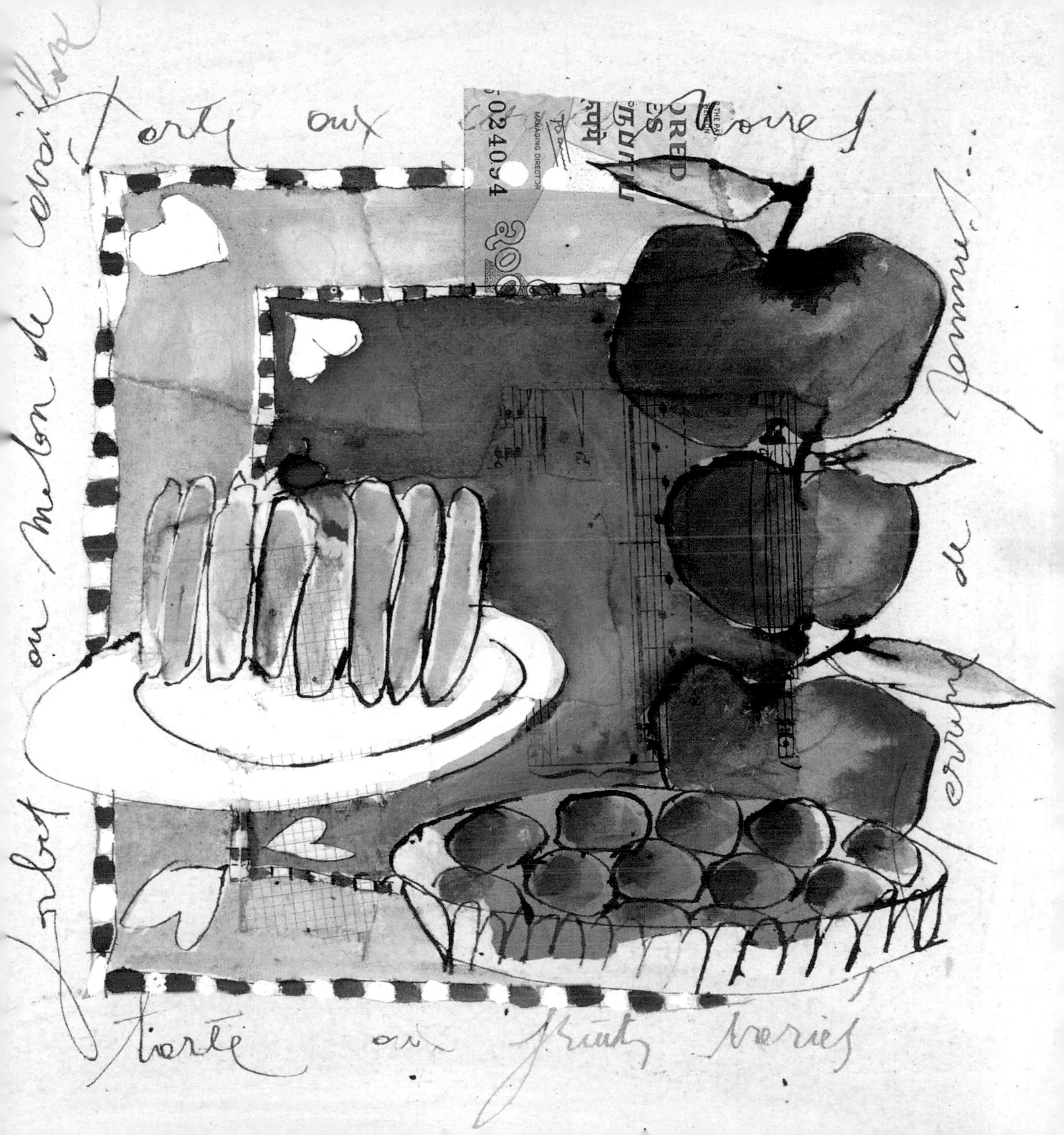
Tarte aux Poires
Sorbet au melon de Cavaillon
crème de pommes...
Tarte aux fruits variés

Les treize desserts provençaux de Noël

The thirteen Provencal Christmas desserts

Ingredients for 6 :
Almonds
Quince jam
Dates
Dry figs
Hazelnut
Walnut
White nougat
Dark nougat
Peers
Apples
Pompe à huile
Plums
Raisins.

Here is the list of the thirteen desserts served on Christmas Eve in the traditional Provencal houses. There are thirteen of them because as this number symbolises Jesus and the twelve apostles.

Nowadays, some people like to replace the dried fruits (called "mendiants" in South of France) by oranges, mandarins, "callissons d'Aix", "oreillettes"… and other delicacies.

Melon de Cavaillon
à la sauce mentholée
Melon with mint sauce

Preparation time :
25 minutes
Cooking time : 3 h for the
melon to marinate

Ingredients for 6 :
2 middle-sized melons (ideally
from Cavaillon)
About 10 fresh leaves of mint.

For the sauce :
1/2 l/1 Pt of whole milk
1 pinch of vanilla
6 egg yolks
100 g/3,5 oz of caster sugar
1 tablespoon of "Grand
Marnier".

Open the melons and remove the seeds. Hollow the flesh out with a teaspoon to form marbles out of it. Throw them in a bowl, and put to one side.

Mix the egg yolks and the sugar in a saucepan and put to one side. Heat up the milk and the vanilla and bring it to the boil. Pour slowly the boiling milk over the eggs and sugar over a slow heat, whisking continuously so that the sauce thickens. Don't let the mixture boil. Away from the heat, add the Grand Marnier, and the chopped leaves of mint, and leave to infuse. Put to one side.

Pour the cold sauce over the melon marbles, stir well and store in a fridge for about 3 hours.

Serve the bowl filled with melon marbles garnished with mint leaves.

This dessert is served chilled. You can prepare it one day beforehand as it will have a stronger flavour. In this case, place it in an airtight container. When buying a melon, you should chose it heavy, as it is a sign of quality.

Nougat glacé aux fruits confits
Chilled nougat and candied fruits

Preparation time :
45 minutes
Ingredients for 6 :
200 g/7 oz
of cooking chocolate
3 eggs
125 g/4 oz of butter
25 g/1 oz of caster sugar
100 g/3,5 oz of half-shelled
walnuts
200 g/7 oz of candied fruits
(cherries and peel of orange)
50 g/2 oz of raisins
1 dl/0,2 Pt of rum
2 tablespoons of "Cointreau"
or orange brandy.

Macerate the raisins in the rum for 15 minutes. Meanwhile, grill the half-shelled walnuts for 10 minutes in a hot oven. Take them out, leave to cool down, and take off most of the skins by rubbing them in your hands. Put to one side.

Finally chop the candied fruits and put them to one side. Melt the chocolate with 2 tablespoons of water over a slow heat, stirring continuously. Add the pieces of butter and mix to get a smooth consistency. Remove the saucepan from the heat.

Mix the egg yolks and 25 g of sugar, with the melted chocolate. Add the candied fruits, the drained raisins, the walnuts and the Cointreau. Give it a stir. Whisk the whites with a pinch of salt and incorporate them to the chocolate preparation.

Pour it in a tin covered with foil, and store in the freezer for at least 3 hours. Turn it over. You can serve this chilled nougat sliced and topped with custard.

Oreillettes de tante Gisèle

Aunt Gisèle's oreillettes

Preparation time :
35 minutes + 1 h for the
batter to stand
Cooking time : 25 minutes

Ingredients for 6 :
450 g/1 lb of flour
125 g/4 oz of butter
3 eggs
The zest of an orange as well
as the zest of a lemon
1/2 cup of orange blossom
water
1.5 l/3 Pt of frying oil
Icing sugar.

Slowly melt the butter in a saucepan, break the eggs in a hollow dish, whisk them and add the melted butter, the orange blossom water, and the zest, as well as the flour, little by little. Knead this mixture until you get a smooth paste. Leave it to stand for at least an hour under a cloth, in a warm place.

Sprinkle the work surface with flour, and share the elastic paste in 50 g pieces. Roll each of them with a rolling pin so as to make them about 2 millimetres thick. Each piece will make one *oreillette*. You can use a pastry wheel to form one or two slits, as it will hasten the cooking process.

Deep fry the *oreillettes* in hot but not boiling oil, and turn them over so as to brown them on both sides. Remove them from the oil, drain them in a sieve and then on kitchen paper, and sprinkle them with icing sugar.

This dessert is very popular in Provence during the Christmas festivities. It is one of the 13 Provencal desserts (see the recipe in the *desserts* chapter) on Christmas Eve. You can knead the paste one day beforehand and store it in the fridge. You can also fry the *oreillettes* a day beforehand as they can be preserved for a few days if you keep them in a dry place.

Petits pavés
aux raisins de Corinthe
Small raisin biscuits

Preparation time :
15 minutes
Cooking time : 5 minutes

Ingredients for 6 :
100 g/3,5 oz of raisins
1 dl/0,2 Pt of rum
120 g/4 oz of butter
120 g/4 oz caster sugar
150 g/5 oz of flour
2 eggs.

Soak the raisins for 10 minutes in the rum. Meanwhile, mix the soft butter with the sugar, the eggs, and the flour so as to get a smooth paste. Add the drained raisins to the preparation and give it a good stir.

Cover the baking tray with greaseproof paper and spread the value of a teaspoon for each biscuit on the baking tray.

Cook the *pavés* for about 5 minutes in the oven. They should hardly brown to stay smooth.

The *pavés* are perfect to be served with a portion of ice-cream, and as they are quick to bake, this recipe is fine when a guest comes unexpected.

Pets de nonne ou beignets soufflés

Pets de nonne or soufflé friters

Preparation time :
10 minutes
Cooking time : 20 minutes

Ingredients for 6 :
250 g/8 oz of flour
1 glass of water
6 eggs
2 handfuls of cooked rice, drained
1 teaspoon of sugar
1 teaspoon of orange blossom water
1 lemon zest
1 pinch of salt
1 l/2 Pt of fresh frying oil.

Pour in a saucepan the water, the chopped butter, the salt and the sugar. Bring to the boil and add the flour, away from the heat, and give it a good stir. Put the saucepan back over a slow heat and stir until the paste doesn't stick to the pan anymore, and remove from the heat.

Then, add the eggs one by one, kneading the paste after each egg has gone in. Pour in the orange blossom water and add the lemon zest and the rice. Put to one side.

Heat up the frying oil and pour a few tablespoons of batter in the hot but not boiling oil. When the fritters are brown on both sides, remove them with a skimmer and drain them on kitchen paper.

Lay the fritters in a dish and sprinkle with sugar.

The *pets de nonne* should be served warm.

Pompes à l'huile

Preparation time :
15 minutes + 3h for the
paste to stand
Cooking time : 30 minutes

Ingredients for 6 :
500 g/1 lb of flour
20 g/1 oz of baking powder
125 g/4 oz of caster sugar
1 dl/0,2 Pt of olive oil
3 tablespoons of orange blossom water
7 to 8 tablespoons of water
25 g/1 oz of grated
orange peel
1 teaspoon of aniseed
Salt.

Dilute the baking powder in 3 tablespoons of warm water in a bowl, and put to one side. In a large mixing bowl, mix the flour, the olive oil, the baking powder, the salt, the sugar, the aniseed, the water, and the orange blossom water. Knead this mixture and leave it to stand for 3 hours in a warm place.

The dough should have doubled in volume. Share it in 3 to 4 equal parts which you should flatten with the hand so that they are round and flat. With the point of a knife, draw any design (an olive branch for example) half a centimetre deep on the *pompes*, and cook them on an oiled baking tray for 25 to 30 minutes in a hot oven.

The *pompes à huile* are served on Christmas Eve in Provence and are one of the thirteen traditional desserts.

Pruneaux d'Agen en salade
Prune salad

Preparation time :
20 minutes + 2 h in the fridge
Cooking time : 15 minutes

Ingredients for 6 :
500 g/1 lb of prunes
1 dried piece of an orange peel (3 or 4 cm long)
2 pinches of vanilla
1 clove
1 pinch of cinnamon
1 pinch of coriander
1 pinch of ground nutmeg
1 dl of rum
1 tablespoon of orange blossom water
40 g/1,5 oz of caster sugar
1/2 l/1 Pt of water.

Throw all the ingredients mentioned apart from the prunes in a saucepan, and simmer for 10 minutes. Throw the prunes in, bring slowly to the boil, and leave to cook for 10 to 15 minutes. Remove the saucepan from the heat, leave the preparation and freeze for 2 hours.

This salad should be served chilled, and can be served with a rice or semolina pudding.

You can also serve it with a custard flavoured with a little honey (add one tablespoon of liquid honey in the custard).

Salade de fruits épicée
Spiced fruit salad

Preparation time :
30 minutes

Ingredients for 6 :
2 bananas
1 apple
2 peers
2 peaches
1 nectarine
1/2 melon
2 handfuls of cherries
1 slice of water melon
3 to 4 apricots
1 bunch of grape
The juice of 3 oranges
2 or 3 vanilla
1 pinch of cinnamon
4 to 5 tablespoons of rum
4 to 5 tablespoons of caster sugar.

Peel all the fruits and remove the stones, apart from the oranges which should be squeezed. Chop the fruits and throw them in a bowl.

Mix the rum and the orange juice, the vanilla, the cinnamon, and the sugar in a food processor. Pour this mixture over the fruits, and store the salad in the fridge.

Serve chilled.

Sauce aux abricots

Apricot sauce

Preparation time :
10 minutes
Cooking time : 10 minutes

Ingredients for 6 :
1 kg/2 lb of apricots
200 g/7 oz of sugar
2 tablespoons of cream
1 dl/0,2 Pt of water
The juice of half a lemon
1 pinch of vanilla
2 tablespoons
of Grand Marnier.

Open the apricots in halves and remove the stones. Throw them in a saucepan with the water, the sugar, the lemon juice, and a pinch of vanilla. Cook them for about 10 minutes. Mix them in the food processor with the cream and the Grand Marnier.

Make sure the sauce is sweet enough (the quantity of sugar you have to add may vary according to the apricots themselves). Leave to cool down.

This sauce is served cold with a vanilla ice-cream, some fromage blanc or a rice pudding.

Sorbet au melon de Cavaillon
Melon sorbet

Preparation time :
10 minutes

Ingredients for 6 :
700 g/1,5 lb of melon (ideally
from Cavaillon)
1/2 l/1 Pt of water
30 cl/0,6 Pt of liquid
cane sugar
1 egg white
3 tablespoons of lemon juice.

Peel the melon and chop it. Mix it in the food processor with the water, the cane sugar, and the lemon juice.

Whisk the egg white, it should be very firm. Mix it with the melon preparation and pour it in the ice cream churn.

Soufflé aux marrons
Chestnut soufflé

Preparation time :
40 minutes
Cooking time :
25 mn + 35 mn to grill the chestnuts.

Ingredients for 6 :
2 dozens of chestnuts
1/4 l/1/2 Pt of milk
2 pinches of vanilla powder
100 g/3,5 lb of caster sugar
125 g/4 lb of butter
3 egg yolks
2 egg whites.

Grill the chestnuts in the oven for 35 minutes. Remove the 2 skins on each fruit. Throw the chestnuts in a saucepan and cover them with milk. Crush them with a fork, add the vanilla, and leave to cook slowly until the milk is totally absorbed, and stir continuously.

Slowly throw in the sugar, stir well and leave the purée to dry totally. Take it away from the heat and add the butter, stirring continuously, and incorporate the egg yolks one after the other, and finally the firm whisked eggs.

Butter a soufflé tin, pour in the preparation and cook au bain marie for 25 minutes in a hot oven. Turn over and serve the soufflé sprinkled with caster sugar immediately.

Tarte sablée aux abricots

Apricot sablé tart

Open the apricots and remove the stones. Put to one side. Mix the flour and the soft butter, the sugar, the egg, the water with a pinch of salt and the vanilla. (The pastry will be better if all the ingredients are at the same temperature.) Slightly knead the pastry until it is dense, but don't over work it. Roll it into a ball, and leave it to stand for 15 to 20 minutes.

Meanwhile, mix the milk, the eggs, the sugar, the cream, the flour, and the vanilla in the food processor.

Roll out the pastry with the pin and lay it in a buttered flan dish. Prick it with a fork, lay in the apricots and pour the filling over it. Sprinkle with sugar. Cook in a hot oven for about 35 minutes. Take the *tarte* out of the oven and sprinkle it one more time with sugar as apricots are always a little acid.

This pie should be served cold.

If you want to remove the apricots acidity, brown them with 100 g of honey in a non-stick pan over a slow heat so that they caramelise a little. Drain them in a sieve before laying them over the pastry.

Preparation time :
20 minutes + 20 minutes
for the pastry to stand.
Cooking time : 35 to 40
minutes

Ingredients for 6 :
1 kg/2 lb of ripe apricot
(I would recommend
the "Polish" variety)

For the pastry :
250 g/8 oz of flour
50 g/2 oz of icing sugar
150 g/5 oz of butter
2 egg yolks
2 tablespoons of water
1 pinch of vanilla

For the filling :
1.5 dl/0,3 Pt of milk
3 eggs
100 g/3,5 oz of sugar
100 g/3,5 oz of cream
1 tablespoon of flour
A pinch of vanilla.

Tarte tatin aux figues fraîches
Fresh fig tatin tart

Preparation time :
30 minutes + 15 minutes
for the pastry to stand
Cooking time : 45 minutes

Ingredients for 6 :
About 15 grey or violet figs
3 to 4 tablespoons of butter
3 tablespoons of caster sugar

For the pastry :
200 g/7 oz of flour
140 g/5 oz of butter
1 whole egg
1 tablespoon of cold water
1 tablespoon of caster sugar
1 pinch of salt
For the caramel :
10 lumps of sugar
1/2 lemon juice
2 tablespoons of water.

Throw in a bowl the flour, the soft butter, the egg, the water, the salt and the sugar. Knead slightly these ingredients until the pastry is dense but smooth. Roll it into a ball and leave it to stand in the fridge for at least 15 minutes.

Meanwhile, melt the butter in a saucepan (ideally a copper pan), sprinkle with sugar, and caramelise slightly. Lay the figs cut into 2 in the dish and cook them in a slow heat for about 25 minutes, taking care to brown them well.

Roll out the pastry (1/2 cm thick) on the floured working surface. Lay the browned figs in a pie plate and cover them with the pastry. Cook in a hot oven for 20 minutes. The tart should be slightly brown. Take it out of the oven, leave it to cool down for a while and turn the tart over so as to see the figs on top of it now.

Make a caramel by melting the sugar, the water and the lemon juice in the saucepan. When it is slightly brown, pour it over the figs and spread it with a fork.

The tart should be served warm, and you can top it with crème fraîche.

Published in spring 2002,
by Grafiche Zanini, Bologna - Italy
to share the modest legacy of this cuisine
of nuances which brings in the plate
the balance of the rural flavours.

3rd edition

Photoengraving by Flashmen, 05000 Gap, France.